The Transparent Society

The Transparent Society

Gianni Vattimo

Translated by David Webb

Polity Press

This English translation © Polity Press 1992
Chapters 1, 2, 3, 4 & 5 first published in Italian as *La società trasparente*
© Garzanti Editore 1989
Chapter 6 first published in Italian in *Fondamenti* 3 (1985)
Chapter 7 first published in Italian in *Micromega* 1 (1986)
Chapter 8 first published in Italian in Gianni Vattimo *Etica dell' interpretazione*
(Turin: Rosenberg & Sellier), 1990
Chapters 6, 7, & 8 © Gianni Vattimo 1992

First published in 1992 by Polity Press
in association with Blackwell Publishers

Editorial office:
Polity Press
65 Bridge Street
Cambridge   CB2 1UR, UK

Marketing and production:
Blackwell Publishers
108 Cowley Road
Oxford   OX4 1JF, UK

All rights reserved. Except for the quotation of short passages for the purposes of criticism and review, no part of this publication may be reproduced, stored in a retrieval system, or transmitted, in any form or by any means, electronic, mechanical, photocopying, recording or otherwise, without the prior permission of the publisher.

Except in the United States of America, this book is sold subject to the condition that it shall not, by way of trade or otherwise, be lent, re-sold, hired out, or otherwise circulated without the publisher's prior consent in any form of binding or cover other than that in which it is published and without a similar condition including this condition being imposed on the subsequent purchaser.

ISBN 0 7456 09260
ISBN 0 7456 10471 (pbk)

A CIP catalogue record for this book is available from the British Library.

Typeset in 12 on 14pt Bembo
by Hope Services (Abingdon) Ltd.
Printed in Great Britain by
T. J. Press (Padstow) Ltd, Padstow, Cornwall

This book is printed on acid-free paper

Contents

1 The Postmodern: A Transparent Society?   1
2 The Human Sciences and the Society of
   Communication   12
3 Myth Rediscovered   28
4 Art and Oscillation   45
5 From Utopia to Heterotopia   62
6 Utopia, Counter-utopia, Irony   76
7 Disenchantment and Dissolution   90
8 Ethics of Communication or Ethics of
   Interpretation?   105
Index   121

1

The Postmodern: A Transparent Society?

Much is said about postmodernity nowadays. So much, in fact, that it has become almost obligatory to distance oneself from the notion, to see it as a fad and to insist on its having been overcome. It is my belief, however, that the term 'postmodern' has a meaning, and that this meaning is linked to the fact that the society in which we live is a society of generalized communication. It is the society of the mass media.

In the first place, we speak of the postmodern because we feel that, in some essential way, modernity is over. To understand what is meant by saying that modernity is over, one must first understand what is meant by modernity. Amongst the many definitions, there is one that may be generally agreed upon: modernity is the epoch in which simply being modern became a decisive value in itself. In Italian, as in many other languages, I believe, it is still an insult to call someone a 'reactionary', that is, attached to values from the past, to tradition, to forms of thought that have been 'overcome'. Broadly speaking, this eulogy to being modern is what, in my view, characterizes the whole of modern culture. It is an attitude that did not really come

The Postmodern: A Transparent Society?

to the fore until the end of the fifteenth century (the 'official' beginning of the modern age), at which point the artist came to be thought of as a creative genius and an increasingly intense cult of the new and original emerged that had not existed before (in previous ages the imitation of models was in fact of the utmost importance). As the centuries passed, it became more and more clear that the cult of the new and original in art was linked to a more general perspective according to which, as in the Enlightenment, human history is seen as an ongoing process of emancipation, as if it were the perfection of the human ideal (the essay 'On the education of the human race' by Lessing is typical in this respect). If history is progressive in this sense, greater value will clearly be attached to that which is more 'advanced', that which is nearer to the conclusion and the end of the process. However, a conception of history as the progressive realization of what is genuinely human requires that it be seen as unilinear. Only if there is History can one speak of progress.

According to the hypothesis I am putting forward, modernity ends when – for a number of reasons – it no longer seems possible to regard history as unilinear. Such a view requires the existence of a centre around which events are gathered and ordered. We think of history as ordered around the year zero of the birth of Christ, and more specifically as a serial train of events in the life of peoples from the 'centre', the West, the place of civilization, outside of which are the 'primitives' and the 'developing' countries. In the nineteenth and twentieth centuries philosophy has launched a radical critique of the idea of unilinear history, exposing the *ideological* character of these views. Thus, in a short essay from 1938 ('Theses on the Philosophy of History'), Walter Benjamin maintained that unilinear

The Postmodern: A Transparent Society?

history is a representation of the past constructed by dominant groups and social classes. Indeed, what is passed on from the past? Not everything that took place, but only that which seems *relevant*. For example, at school we studied the dates of battles, peace treaties and even revolutions, but they never told us of radical changes in forms of nutrition, or in sexual attitudes, or things of that kind. History speaks only of events involving those who count, the nobles, the sovereigns, or the middle classes once they became powerful. The poor, and those aspects of life considered 'base', do not 'make history'.

If observations such as these are developed further (along a path cleared before Benjamin by Marx and Nietzsche), the idea of unilinear history ends up being dissolved. There is no single history, only images of the past projected from different points of view. It is illusory to think that there exists a supreme or comprehensive viewpoint capable of unifying all others (such as 'History', encompassing the histories of art, of literature, of wars, of sexuality, etc.).

With the crisis in the idea of history comes a second crisis in the idea of progress: if human events do not make up a unilinear continuum, then one cannot regard them as proceeding towards an end, realizing a rational programme of improvement, education and emancipation. Moreover, the end that modernity took to be giving direction to the course of events was itself drawn according to a certain ideal of man. More or less all Enlightenment thinkers, Hegel, Marx, positivists, historians of every type, considered the meaning of history to be the realization of civilization, that is, of the form of Western European man. Just as history may be thought as unilinear only from the point of view of one placed at the centre (whether this be the coming of Christ or the

The Postmodern: A Transparent Society?

Holy Roman Empire), so the conception of progress requires a certain ideal of man as its criterion. In modernity, however, the criterion has always been that of modern European man – as if to say: we Europeans are the best form of humanity and the entire course of history is directed towards the more or less complete realization of this ideal.

Bearing this in mind, one appreciates that the present crisis in the unilinear conception of history and consequently the crisis in the idea of progress and the end of modernity are not determined by transformations in theory alone – by the critiques undergone by nineteenth-century historicism (idealist, positivist, Marxist, etc.) at the level of ideas. What has happened is something quite different and of far greater magnitude: the so-called 'primitive' peoples colonized by Europeans in the good and rightful name of 'superior' and more evolved civilization have rebelled, making a unilinear and centralized history *de facto* problematic. The European ideal of humanity has been revealed as one ideal amongst others, not necessarily worse, but unable, without violence, to obtain as the true essence of man, of all men.

Along with the end of colonialism and imperialism, another decisive factor in both the dissolution of the idea of history and the end of modernity is the advent of the society of communication. Here I come to my second point, which concerns the 'transparent society'. It will not have gone unnoticed that the expression 'transparent society' has been introduced here with a question mark. What I am proposing is: (a) that the mass media play a decisive role in the birth of a postmodern society; (b) that they do not make this postmodern society more 'transparent', but more complex, even chaotic; and finally (c) that it is in precisely this relative 'chaos' that our hopes for emancipation lie.

The Postmodern: A Transparent Society?

The impossibility of thinking history as unilinear – an impossibility that, according to the thesis put forward here, lays the basis for the end of modernity – does not derive solely from the crisis in European colonialism and imperialism. It is also, and perhaps above all, the result of the birth of means of mass communication. These means – newspapers, radio, television, what is now called telematics – have been decisive in bringing about the dissolution of centralized perspectives, of what the French philosopher Jean-François Lyotard calls the 'grand narratives'. This view of the effect of the mass media seems to be the very contrary of that taken by the philosopher Theodor Adorno. On the basis of his experience in the United States during the Second World War, Adorno, in works such as *The Dialectic of Enlightenment* (written with Max Horkheimer) and *Minima Moralia*, predicted that radio (and only later TV) would produce a general homogenization of society. By virtue of a kind of innate propensity for the demonic, this in turn would permit and indeed favour the formation of dictatorships and totalitarian governments capable, like 'Big Brother' in George Orwell's *Nineteen Eighty Four*, of exercising widespread control over their citizens by the diffusion of slogans, propaganda (commercial as well as political) and stereotypical world views. Instead, what actually happened, in spite of the efforts of the monopolies and major centres of capital, was that radio, television and newspapers became elements in a general explosion and proliferation of *Weltanschauungen*, of world views. Recent decades in the United States have seen minorities of every kind take to the microphones. Cultures and subcultures of all sorts have stepped into the limelight of public opinion. Of course, one could object that having a voice does not correspond to true political emancipation – economic power is still held by capital. This may be so: I won't pursue the issue here. But the fact remains that the very logic of the information 'market' requires its continual expansion, and consequently demands that 'everything' somehow become an object of communication. This giddy proliferation of communication as more and more subcultures 'have their say' is the most obvious effect of the mass media. Together with the end, or at least radical transformation, of European imperialism, it is also the key to our society's shift towards postmodernity. The West is living through an explosive situation, not only with regard to other cultural universes (such as the 'third world'), but internally as well, as an apparently irresistible pluralization renders any unilinear view of the world and history impossible.

This is why the society of the mass media should be contrasted sharply with a more enlightened, more 'educated', society (in the sense intended by Lessing, or Hegel, or even Comte or Marx). The mass media, which in theory offer information in 'real time' about everything happening in the world, could in effect be seen as a kind of concrete realization of Hegel's Absolute Spirit: the perfect self-consciousness of the whole of humanity, the coincidence between what happens, history and human knowledge. On close inspection, Hegelian and Marxist critics such as Adorno work with this model in mind, and their pessimism is based on the fact that it is not realized as it might have been (owing to the market, ultimately), or is realized only in a perverse and caricatural form (as in the sanctioned world of 'Big Brother', which may even be 'happy', thanks to the manipulation of desires). But the freedom given by the mass media to so many cultures and *Weltanschauungen* has belied the very ideal of a transparent society. What could freedom of information, or even the existence of

The Postmodern: A Transparent Society?

more than one radio or TV channel, mean in a world where the norm is the exact reproduction of reality, perfect objectivity, the complete identity of map and territory? In actual fact, the increase in possible information on the myriad forms of reality makes it increasingly difficult to conceive of a *single* reality. It may be that in the world of the mass media a 'prophecy' of Nietzsche's is fulfilled: in the end the true world becomes a fable. If we, in late modernity, have an idea of reality, it cannot be understood as the objective given lying beneath, or beyond, the images we receive of it from the media. How and where could we arrive at such a reality 'in itself'? For us, reality is rather the result of the intersection and 'contamination' (in the Latin sense) of a multiplicity of images, interpretations and reconstructions circulated by the media in competition with one another and without any 'central' coordination.

The view I want to put forward is that in the media society, the ideal of emancipation modelled on lucid self-consciousness, on the perfect knowledge of one who knows how things stand (compare Hegel's Absolute Spirit or Marx's conception of man freed from ideology), is replaced by an ideal of emancipation based on oscillation, plurality and, ultimately, on the erosion of the very 'principle of reality'. Humanity today can finally become aware that perfect freedom is not that described by Spinoza, and does not lie in having a perfect knowledge of the necessary structure of reality and conforming to it – as metaphysics has always dreamt. This is where the philosophical lessons learnt from Nietzsche and Heidegger are most important. For they have provided us with the means to understand the emancipatory significance of the end of modernity and of its idea of history. Nietzsche showed the image of reality as a well-founded rational order (the perennial metaphysical image of the world) to be only the 'reassuring' myth of a still primitive and barbaric humanity. Metaphysics is a violent response to a situation that is itself fraught with danger and violence. It seeks to master reality at a stroke, grasping (or so it thinks) the first principle on which all things depend (and thus giving itself an empty guarantee of power over events). Following Nietzsche in this respect, Heidegger showed that to think of being as foundation, and reality as a rational system of causes and effects, is simply to extend the model of 'scientific' objectivity to the totality of being. All things are reduced to the level of pure presences that can be measured, manipulated, replaced and therefore easily dominated and organized – and in the end man, his interiority and historicity are all reduced to the same level.

If the proliferation of images of the world entails that we lose our 'sense of reality', as the saying goes, perhaps it's not such a great loss after all. By a perverse kind of internal logic, the world of objects measured and manipulated by techno-science (the world of the *real*, according to metaphysics) has become the world of merchandise and images, the phantasmagoria of the mass media. Should we counterpose to this world the nostalgia for a solid, unitary, stable and 'authoritative' reality? In its effort to reconstruct the world of our infancy, where familial authority was both a threat and a comfort, such nostalgia is in continual danger of turning into neurosis.

But what exactly might this loss of reality, this genuine erosion of the principle of reality, mean for emancipation and liberation? Emancipation, here, consists in *disorientation*, which is at the same time also the liberation of differences, of local elements, of what could generally be called dialect. With the demise of the

The Postmodern: A Transparent Society?

idea of a central rationality of history, the world of generalized communication explodes like a multiplicity of 'local' rationalities – ethnic, sexual, religious, cultural or aesthetic minorities – that finally speak up for themselves. They are no longer repressed and cowed into silence by the idea of a single true form of humanity that must be realized irrespective of particularity and individual finitude, transience and contingency. Incidentally, the liberation of differences does not necessarily mean the surrender of every rule or the manifestation of brute immediacy. Dialects have grammar and syntax too, and indeed only discover them when they become visible and acquire a dignity of their own. With the liberation of diversity, they 'find their voice', present themselves and so 'get into shape' for recognition; this is anything but a manifestation of brute immediacy.

The emancipatory effect of the liberation of local rationalities is not confined to guaranteeing everyone the possibility of greater recognition and 'authenticity', as if emancipation meant finally showing what everyone – black, woman, homosexual, Protestant, etc. – 'really' is (to use terms that are still metaphysical, Spinozan).

The emancipatory significance of the liberation of differences and dialects consists rather in the general *disorientation* accompanying their initial identification. If, in a world of dialects, I speak my own dialect, I shall be conscious that it is not the only 'language', but that it is precisely one amongst many. If, in this multicultural world, I set out my system of religious, aesthetic, political and ethnic values, I shall be acutely conscious of the historicity, contingency and finiteness of these systems, starting with my own.

Nietzsche, in *The Gay Science*, called this 'continuing to dream knowing one is dreaming'. But is such a thing possible? This is the essence of what Nietzsche called the 'overman' (or beyond-man), the *Übermensch*: and he assigns the task of attaining it to mankind of the future, in the world of intensified communication.

The significance of the emanicipatory 'confusion' of dialects is exemplified in Dilthey's description of aesthetic experience (a description that is decisive also for Heidegger, in my view). For Dilthey, to encounter a work of art (or indeed to acquire historical knowledge), was to experience in the imagination forms of existence and ways of life different from the one in which we have become immersed in our own concrete everydayness. As we grow older, we all narrow our horizons of life, specializing in one thing or another and enclosing ourselves within a particular circle of friendships, interests and acquaintances. Aesthetic experience leads us into other possible worlds, and we are made to realize the contingency and relativity of the 'real' world in which we have to live.

In the society of generalized communication and the plurality of cultures, the encounter with other worlds and forms of life is perhaps less in the imagination than it was for Dilthey. 'Other' possibilities of existence are realized before our very eyes, in the multiplicity of 'dialects' and in the different cultural universes opened up by anthropology and ethnology. To live in this pluralistic world means to experience freedom as a continual oscillation between belonging and disorientation.

Such freedom is problematic. As an effect of the media, it cannot be guaranteed and remains a possibility still to be recognized and taken up (the media can always and everywhere be the voice of 'Big Brother', or of stereotypical banality, void of meaning . . .). Moreover, we ourselves still do not have a clear idea of its

The Postmodern: A Transparent Society?

physiognomy and so have difficulty in seeing oscillation as freedom. Individually and collectively, we still have a deep-seated nostalgia for the reassuring, yet manacing, closure of horizons. Nihilistic philosophers such as Nietzsche and Heidegger (but also pragmatists like Dewey or Wittgenstein), in demonstrating that being does not necessarily coincide with what is stable, fixed and permanent, but has instead to do with the event, with consensus, dialogue and interpretation, are trying to show us how to take the experience of oscillation in the postmodern world as an opportunity of a new way of being (finally, perhaps) human.

2

The Human Sciences and the Society of Communication

The relation between the human sciences and the society of communication – today's society characterized by an intensification in the exchange of information and the tendency to equate (via television) 'event' with 'news item' – is closer and more organic than is generally realized. Indeed, if in general the sciences in their modern experimental and 'technical' form (as the manipulation of natural data) *constitute* their object as opposed to exploring a 'reality' already constituted and ordered beforehand, this is especially true of the human sciences. These are not simply a new way of addressing an 'external' and unchanging phenomenon, namely, humanity and its institutions. Rather, their methods and cognitive ideal were made possible by changes in individual and collective life, and by a kind of social existence itself shaped directly by forms of modern communication. The possibility of sociology as the science, or prediction, of collective behaviour, or even as a typology of differences in such behaviour, depends on our ability to gather the necessary information (which presupposes a certain form of communication). Above all, however, something like collective behaviour must first have been established; and this can only happen once a certain level of social communication has been reached. Anthropological knowledge is especially dependent on the possibility of contact with different civilizations and groups of people – contact that only took place in a significant sense with the travel and discoveries of the modern age. Turning to sociology and the context of modern social change, a description of society other than a catalogue and comparison of political regimes (such as we find in Aristotle's *Politics*), would have been inconceivable prior to the constitution of something like 'society', that is, what Hegel called civil society as distinct from the State and the formal political organization of power. To be sure, the connection between the rise and development of civil society as distinct from the State on the one hand and the phenomena of communication and the new means of information made available by modern technology on the other is not immediately obvious. Nonetheless, it can be shown – see, for example, Habermas's work on this topic[1] – that public opinion and the general idea of a public sphere play a fundamental role in the evolution of civil society as a domain distinct from the State. This is undoubtedly linked to the mechanisms of information and social communication.

We could begin by saying – although this requires more careful analysis – that the so-called human sciences (a term whose limits and scope are somewhat indefinite here, as in contemporary culture generally), from sociology and anthropology through to psychology (all of which have in fact emerged only in modernity), and the constitution of modern society as the society of communication reciprocally determine one another. The human sciences both follow from and promote the development of the society of generalized communication.

Human Sciences and Society of Communication

Although an exhaustive definition of either the human sciences or the society of communication is impossible, precisely by virtue of their initial transparency in contemporary culture, it is generally agreed that the human sciences comprise those branches of knowledge that make up what Kant called pragmatic anthropology (or that tend to do so, for example psychology). These give a 'positive', as opposed to a transcendental–philosophical, description of humanity, taking as their basis not what humanity is by nature, but rather what it has made of itself, that is to say, its institutions, culture and symbolic forms. To be sure, such a definition of the human sciences leaves many problems outstanding, especially in connection with the anthropology of Arnold Gehlen. What interests us here, however, is not so much an epistemologically exhaustive definition of the human sciences as the relation between these forms of knowledge (wherever their exact boundaries may lie) and the society of generalized communication. If we float the general hypothesis that the human sciences are those which give a 'positive' description of what humanity makes of itself in culture and society, we can see that the very idea of such a description is essentially conditioned by the unfolding, in a manner accessible to comparative analysis, of the positivity of the human phenomenon. This occurs most clearly in the development of the communicative aspects of modern society.

Yet, to speak of a society of communication implies a further hypothesis, adding scope and complexity to our first on the connection between such a society and the human sciences. The intensification of communicative phenomena and the increasingly prominent circulation of information, with news flashed around the world (or McLuhan's 'global village') as it happens, are not merely aspects of modernization amongst others, but in some way the centre and the very sense of this process. This hypothesis obviously recalls McLuhan's theory that a society may be defined according to the technologies it has at its disposal. In this case, it is not meant generally, but in the specific sense of technologies of communication. In speaking of a 'Gutenberg Galaxy', therefore, we draw attention not merely to one aspect, however essential, of modern and contemporary societies, but rather to the essential character of these two types of society. We have to realize that when we speak of a technical civilization, in the broadest and most 'ontological' sense implied by Heidegger's notion of the *Ge-stell*, this does not mean simply the sum of all the technical apparatus that mediates man's relation to nature and eases his existence by making every conceivable use of natural forces. Although this definition of technology generally holds good for all ages, today it appears too generic and superficial. The technology that shapes the world we live in is indeed made up of machines, in the traditional sense of the word, which provide us with the means to 'dominate' external nature. But it is primarily and essentially defined by systems collecting and transmitting information. This becomes increasingly obvious as the gap between developed and underdeveloped countries is gradually revealed as a gap in the development of information technology. Consequently, when Heidegger defines modernity with reference to an 'age of the world-picture',[2] he is neither being metaphorical, nor singling out a particular feature of the techno-scientific complex fundamental to modern thinking. Rather, he defines modernity as that epoch in which the world is reduced to – or constituted as – images; not *Weltanschauungen* as value systems and subjective points of view, objects of a possible 'psychology of world views', but images constructed and verified by science. These images take shape in the course of both the manipulation of experiments and the application of results to experimental techniques, and (something that Heidegger does not make clear) culminate in the science and technology of information.

Accordingly, to say that modern society is essentially the society of communication and the social sciences does not mean placing in parentheses the significance of the natural sciences and the technology they have made possible in the determination of the structure of this society. It means, rather, that: (a) the 'sense' in which technology moves is not so much the mechanical domination of nature as the development specifically of information and the construction of the world as 'images'; (b) this society is not only that in which technology has reached its peak, but is also, and essentially, the society of the human sciences – in both senses of the genitive. On the one hand, the society is known and constructed by the human sciences as their proper object; on the other, it is distinguished by the fact that it expresses itself through these sciences.

This set of hypotheses could be corroborated, if not proved, by showing that they provide a way of understanding the centrality of information technologies in late-industrial society, that is, their role as the 'organ of organs', the site of the technological complex's 'pilot' or cybernaut, its direction, and a potential direction for its development. As an overarching hypothesis, this unitary description of the technological world as a world of the social sciences and information technology may also help define the 'contemporaneity' of the contemporary world. According to the view we have put forward, the latter is called this not on the basis of banal criteria of 'chronological' proximity (that which is temporally closest to us is contemporary), but rather because it is a world in which a potential reduction of history to the level of simultaneity, via technology such as live television news bulletins, is becoming ever more real.

This definition of contemporaneity undoubtedly entails a radical revision of the very notion of history. Yet one does not have to follow this hypothesis through to its most extreme and dizzy consequences to see the plausibility of another point linked to this hypothesis: in its light, the social ideals of modernity may in each case be described as guided by the utopia of absolute *self-transparency*. Since the Enlightenment, if not before, it has been clear that the subjection of elements of human reality – institutions, culture, psychology, morals – to scientific analysis is not merely an epistemological programme for the pursuit of the interests of knowledge and the extension of scientific method into new areas of study. It is a revolutionary decision that can only be understood in relation to the ideal of a radical transformation of society. This is not to say that we should consider knowledge of humanity and its institutions as a means towards their more effective modification. The Enlightenment is neither a stage of nor a prelude to emancipation, but rather its very essence. In the society of the human sciences, the human has finally become the object of rigorous, valid and verifiable scientific knowledge. The importance attached to qualities such as tolerance and freedom of speech by the programme of Enlightenment emancipation does not derive simply, or even principally, from their being part of a more general demand for freedom. The motive lies rather in the conscious awareness that a free society is one in which humanity can reach self-awareness in a 'public sphere', namely that of public opinion, open discussion etc., unimpaired by dogmatism, prejudice and superstition. Positivistic 'scientism', expressed concretely in the call for the knowledge of humanity to move on to a positive phase, cannot be reduced to a banal overvaluation of the methodology of the natural sciences, the application of which to social and moral issues would then endow these branches of knowledge with greater certainty and efficacy. Instead, at least as far as Comte is concerned, it can only be understood by analogy with the Hegelian programme of the 'realization' of Absolute Spirit and the full self-transparency of reason.

This ideal of self-transparency, according to which social communication and the human sciences are not merely instrumental with regard to the programme of emancipation but in some way concern its very end and substance, is widespread in social theory today and is typified by the thought of authors such as Jürgen Habermas and Karl Otto Apel. In different ways, each of them stands in the legacy of critical Marxism, hermeneutics and the philosophy of language. Above all, however, they are both strongly influenced by neo-Kantianism in association with a certain interpretation of psychoanalysis. Apel, for example, constructs his entire vision of society and morality around the ideal (in place of a Kantian categorical imperative) of the 'community of unlimited communication' – a formulation that goes back to Peirce, and to which he gives the function of a meta-rule that makes all our various language games possible.[3] Recalling Wittgenstein's famous aphorism that one cannot play a language game by oneself, Apel sees in every use of language, and thus in every act of thought, an implicit and ineluctable assumption of responsibility with respect to linguistic rules. Moreover, this responsibility binds speakers to partners, real or potential, before whom each is responsible for respecting the rules. This is true even when playing entirely private games with languages made up solely for oneself; for in this case, the speaker who invents the rules is not identical with the speaker who then, in a different moment, applies them and who assumes responsibility before some potential partner for observing them correctly. This means, however, that every linguistic act takes place within the horizon of an ideal community of speakers, to whom the subject – if his playing the linguistic game is to have any sense – cannot help but assign the same rights as he assigns himself. Hence, there is a kind of intrinsic requirement that language be truthful, which in turn requires the removal of every obstacle to the complete transparency of communication; above all, those set voluntarily (by subjects who then cannot help recognizing that they should have acted differently, as indeed happens in every case of disregard for moral imperatives), but also all those various kinds of social, ideological and psychological obstacles that actually make communication opaque and imperfect. We have here an extension and radicalization of what Peirce called 'logical socialism', an expression that sheds much light on the normative ideal at the bottom of this discourse: the ideal of perfect transparency in knowledge, a transformation of society into a kind of scientific 'subject' – akin to the scientist in the laboratory who is without prejudices, or is at least able to prescind from them for the sake of an objective measurement of the facts. For Apel, then, the human or social sciences are a decisive moment in the realization of a logical socialism. They are in fact the positive condition of possibility for a social self-consciousness surpassing the limits of both idealism and materialist determinism. The dialectic of these two moments operates, in view of their synthesis and overcoming, precisely

> at the moment when the community of communication, which constitutes the transcendental subject of science, becomes at the same time the object of science, in the field of the social sciences in the broadest sense of the term. It now becomes clear that on the one hand, the subject of possible consensus over the truth of science is not an otherworldly 'consciousness in general', but the real-historical society; on the other hand, the real-historical society can only be comprehended adequately if it is treated as a virtual subject of science, including the social sciences, and if its historical reality is in each case reconstructed, in a manner both empirical and critical-normative, with reference to the ideal of realizing the community of unrestricted communication in society.[4]

The term 'community', besides taking up a theme from Peirce, evokes a communication that is more organic and immediate, and we can begin to see that its introduction changes the expression 'a society of communication' from a generic description into a normative ideal. In so doing, it marks out one of the directions taken by Apel, namely that towards a sort of pervasive romantic ideal which is often predominant in contemporary theories of communication.[5] The society of unrestricted communication in which the community of logical socialism is realized is a transparent society. It manages radically to reduce motives for conflict, precisely by eliminating obstacles and opacity via a process modelled loosely on a certain ideal of psychoanalysis.

Apel's theses are significant not only because they assign an essential role to the human sciences in realizing a society of communication taken as a normative ideal, but also because they cast an unequivocal light on what is essential in this ideal, namely the potentially complete self-transparency of society. Such society would be the subject–object of a reflexive knowledge that in some sense realized the absoluteness of spirit which for Hegel remained a purely ideological chimera, an 'ideal' absoluteness related to concrete reality by a 'Platonic' transcendence typical of metaphysical essences, with all their implications – including those that were, broadly speaking, repressive (insofar as they necessarily remained transcendental). The importance of this ideal of self-transparency for contemporary culture is confirmed by the conceptual structure of Sartre's extensive research into dialectic reason. Here the problem is precisely that of individuating the concrete means for establishing society's self-knowledge in non-alienated forms, in order that all members of society may participate. Sartre naturally thinks of revolution, whereas Habermas and Apel think of the emancipatory implications of the social sciences. However, the ideal of self-transparency is the same.

Is it towards this ideal of self-transparency, then, that the conjunction of the social sciences and the society of communication is pointing today? Are we finally in a position to bring about a world in which, as Sartre says in *Search for a Method*, the meaning of history will dissolve into those who make it concrete?[6] Such a possibility does in fact seem to be within reach. The mass media, by means of which society's self-knowledge is transmitted to all its members, have only to prevent themselves being conditioned by ideologies, vested interests etc., and to become somehow 'organs' of the social sciences, submitting to the critical measure of a rigorous knowledge and spreading the 'scientific' image of society that the human sciences are now capable of constructing.

If we measure the present situation against such a prospect of the normative ideal of self-transparency, we are faced with a series of paradoxical facts: the same facts, for example, as those encountered by contemporary historians. As Nicola Tranfaglia writes,

> paradoxically, just as huge developments in communication and the exchange of cultural as well as political information made a genuinely worldwide project of history possible, the decline of Europe and the birth of thousands of other centres of history nullified that possibility and forced Western and European historiography to confront the necessity of a profound change in its conception of the world.[7]

In general, the intense development of the human sciences and the intensification of social communication do not seem to produce a growth in the self-transparency of society. Indeed, they seem to have the opposite effect. Is it simply – as a critical sociology following too uncritically in the footsteps of nineteenth-century *Zivilisations-Kritik* often seems to suppose – that technological innovation has an intrinsic tendency to prop up the powers that be, becoming fatally enslaved to propaganda, advertising and the preservation and intensification of ideology? Yet, it seems that the impossibility faced by contemporary historians of constructing a universal history is principally bound up not so much with limits of this kind, as with reasons of a quite contrary sort; there is a kind of entropy linked to the very proliferation of the centres of history, that is, of the places where information is gathered, unified and transmitted. From this perspective, the idea of a world history is revealed as what it has in fact always been, namely a reduction of the train of human events from a single perspective which is in each case a function of domination, whether class-based or colonial, etc. Something of the kind probably holds for the ideal of society's self-transparency as well. Although it only works from the point of view of a central subject, such a subject becomes ever more unthinkable with each advance in the technology that should make its realization 'possible'. Perhaps this is the destiny contemporary society reserves for Hegelianism, for the *Aufklärung*, or what Heidegger calls metaphysics. As the self-transparency of society becomes possible from a purely technical point of view, this self-transparency is shown to be an ideal of domination and not emancipation, as demonstrated by Adorno's sociological critique. At the same time – and this is what Adorno missed – within the communication system itself, mechanisms develop (the 'rise of new centres of history') that make the realization of self-transparency in principle impossible.

The debate over the 'scientific' credentials of the human sciences that has figured so prominently in twentieth-century culture should, I believe, be reconsidered in the light of this hypothesis. As we know, the origins of this debate, in the course of which the human sciences first defined their own specific physiognomy, were marked by the distinction (made by Windelband) between natural nomothetic sciences and human ideographic sciences (or, in Dilthey, between causal explanation in the natural sciences and 'comprehension' in the human sciences). This opposition was unsatisfactory from the very beginning, and has never appeared more so than in recent decades; not merely because the human sciences cannot be left at the mercy of an almost exclusively intuitive and empathic understanding, but above all because it has become clear that the natural sciences are themselves determined by historico-cultural models, which in turn end up including the supposedly 'neutral' model of causal explanation as well. However things stand with the natural sciences, the human sciences are undoubtedly structured by cognitive schemes – from that based on the Weberian ideal-type to Cassirer's reliance on the historical-normative notion of style (taken up again by Wölfflin),[8] to Popper's 'zero-model'[9] – whose intra-historical character typifies the interpretative models adopted by the human sciences. This intra-historical character keeps the human sciences from seeing themselves as entirely reflexive, that is, as capable of reflecting reality independently of interpretative schemes that are themselves historical, and therefore neither innovative nor a pure mirror for that which is to be objectively known. But that is not all. This hermeneutic taking stock, as it were, has led the human sciences to recognize the historical, limited and ultimately ideological character of the ideal of self-transparency, no less than that of universal history mentioned earlier. Apel's and Habermas's ideal of a community of unrestricted communication is undoubtedly modelled on the community of researchers and scientists to which Peirce referred when speaking of logical socialism. But can one legitimately model the emancipated human subject, and ultimately society, on the ideal of the scientist in her laboratory, whose objectivity and disinterest are demanded by what is at bottom a technological interest and who conceives of nature as an object only to the extent that it is marked out as a place for potential domination – thereby implying a series of ideals, expectations and motives under widespread criticism today?

Instead of moving towards self-transparency, the society of the human sciences and generalized communication has moved towards what could, in general, be called the 'fabling of the world'. The images of the world we receive from the media and the human sciences, albeit on different levels, are not simply different interpretations of a 'reality' that is 'given' regardless, but rather constitute the very objectivity of the world. 'There are no facts, only interpretations', in the words of Nietzsche, who also wrote that 'the true world has in the end become a fable'.[10]

To be sure, there is no sense in purely and simply denying the world a 'unitary reality', in a kind of reprise of naive empirical idealism. It makes more sense to recognize that what we call the 'reality of the world' is the 'context' for the multiplicity of 'fablings' – and the task and significance of the human sciences lie precisely in thematizing the world in these terms.

In this sense, the *methodological* debate that occupies such a considerable part of the human sciences today, however empty it may seem at times, is not merely instrumental and preliminary, but represents a central and substantial moment of these sciences. At the very least it helps to make them undogmatic, turning them into 'fables' aware of their own 'fabulous' character. The recent good fortune enjoyed by the notion of narrative in the discussions of historians and sociologists, and the enquiry into 'rhetorical' and narratological models of historiography, are very much part of this picture of a form of knowledge belonging to the human sciences that critically eliminates the myth of transparency: in favour not of a totally relativistic scepticism, but of a less ideological openness to experience of the world. In turn, the world is not so much the object of tendentially (but always only tendentially) 'objective' knowledge, as the place where symbolic systems are produced. These are distinct from myths precisely insofar as they are 'historical', that is, are narrations that have a critical distance and are aware of the coordinate-systems in which they are situated. They know themselves to be, and present themselves explicitly as, 'having-become' and never pretend to be 'nature'.

Once thought acknowledges the fabling of the world, albeit in the specific sense referred to here, the problem of its critical status naturally becomes a matter of urgent concern. At present there are only a few clear points of reference. Above all, the logic on the basis of which knowledge in the human sciences and the possible 'truth' of the world of media-ized communication can be described and critically evaluated is a 'hermeneutic' logic that seeks truth as continuity, 'correspondence', dialogue between texts, and not as the conformity of what is said to some mythical state of affairs. This logic is all the more rigorous the less it lets itself be taken over by a particular system of symbols, or a certain 'narration'. In this respect, the term 'hermeneutics' retains its reference to the 'school of suspicion' (to use another of Nietzsche's expressions). If we cannot pretend (any longer?) to unveil the lies of ideologies and strike an ultimate stable foundation, we can still emphasize the plurality of 'tales' and put it to use in freeing ourselves from both the inflexibility of monological tales and the dogmatic systems of myth.

The self-transparency to which we are at present being led by the ensemble of media and human sciences seems to be nothing more than the exposure of pluralism, of the mechanisms and inner fabric of our culture. Even at its best, the media–human sciences complex is emancipatory only inasmuch as it places us in a world less univocal, less certain and so also much less reassuring than that of myth. It is the world for which Nietzsche invented the figure of the *Übermensch*, the overman, a new human subject capable of living without neurosis; the same world to which philosophy responds by way of what may now justifiably be called the hermeneutic turn.

NOTES

1. Cf. J. Habermas, *Strukturwandel der Offentlichkeit* (Luchterhand Verlag, Neuwied, 1962).
2. M. Heidegger, 'The age of the world-picture', in *The Question Concerning Technology and Other Essays*, tr. W. Lovitt (Harper & Row, New York, 1977), pp. 115–54.
3. Cf. K. O. Apel, *Transformation der Philosophie*, 2 vols. (Suhrkamp Verlag, Frankfurt a. M., 1973).
4. Ibid., vol. 2, p. 225.
5. Cf. G. Vattimo, 'L'ermeneutica e il modello della communità', in U. Curi (ed.), *La communicazione umana* (Angeli, Milan, 1985).
6. Cf. J.-P. Sartre, *Search for a Method* (1960), tr. H. Barnes (Random House, New York), pp. 76–7.
7. In the Introduction to vol. 10, 2 of N. Tranfaglia (ed.), *Il mondo contemporaneo* (La Nuova Italia, Florence, 1983).
8. For example, E. Cassirer, *The Logic of the Humanities* (1942), tr. C. Smith Howe (Yale University Press, New Haven, Conn., 1961).
9. K. R. Popper, *The Poverty of Historicism* (1944–5) (Ark, London, 1986).
10. [Translation modified – Trans.] This is the title of a chapter from *Twilight of the Idols* (1888), tr. R. J. Hollingdale (Penguin Books, Harmondsworth, 1968).

3

Myth Rediscovered

One of the most urgent problems faced by contemporary consciousness as it becomes aware of how the world is 'fabled' by the media and the social sciences is that of redefining its own position with regard to myth. This is above all to avoid the (common) conclusion that the appropriate response to the question 'What does thinking mean?' in late modernity lies precisely in a rediscovery of myth.

In contemporary philosophy there is no satisfactory theory of myth, of its essence and its links with other forms of relation to the world. Yet the notion of myth, though ill-defined, has a wide circulation in current culture. Roland Barthes's 'Myth Today' spawned, or reinforced, a general tendency to analyse mass culture and its products in terms of mythology. While Sorel's *Reflexions sur la violence* provided a remote but nonetheless serviceable basis for the continuing presence, indeed the necessity, of myth in politics as an agent capable of moving the masses. Even Lévi-Strauss, whose anthropological treatment of myth is highly technical, suggests in *Structural Anthropology* that nothing resembles mythical thought more than political ideology. In

Myth Rediscovered

today's society, the latter has in a certain way simply replaced the former.[1] Although Lévi-Strauss could hardly be accused of using the term 'myth' imprecisely, such a statement, even by him, does reflect the common, non-technical, usage of the term 'myth' and so contributes to the vagueness just mentioned. In fact, when, in the later *Introduction to a Science of Mythology*, Lévi-Strauss brings a more precise conception of myth to the question of its survival in the modern world, it is in music and literature that he identifies the elements and forms of experience in which myth survives, albeit weakened.[2] However, it is not to this more limited and technical sense of the term that one refers in talking of myth's presence in our culture, but rather to a vaguer sense wherein myth is understood roughly as follows: unlike scientific thought, myth is not demonstrative or analytic etc., but narrative and fantastic, playing on the emotions with little or no pretence to objectivity. It concerns religion and art, ritual and magic.

Science, on the other hand, is born in opposition to it as a demythologization and 'disenchantment of the world'.

> Wherever philosophy sought to establish a theoretical view of the world, it was confronted not so much by immediate phenomenal reality as by the mythical transformation of this reality . . . Long before the world appeared to consciousness as a totality of empirical things and a complex of empirical attributes it was manifested as an aggregate of mythical powers and effects.[3]

In this quotation from Cassirer's 1923 book, which is perhaps the last great theoretical treatment of myth in our century, one can clearly see an implicit and essential feature of the modern theory of myth, namely the idea that its knowledge is 'prior' to that of science, more ancient and less mature, bound more to infantile and adolescent traits in the history of the human mind. Lévi-Strauss by no means shares the flatly evolutionary conception according to which myth is destined to develop into *logos*, and indeed he presents himself as a radical antihistoricist. Yet even he considers myth to belong to our culture's past, and is at pains to identify both its surrogate in political ideology and the traces it has left in music and literature.

However, drawing out these implications of Cassirer's and Lévi-Strauss's views, not to mention Weber's, leaves us feeling uneasy. The basis of this unease is quite straightforward: modern philosophical theories of myth, up to the most recent, namely Cassirer's, have always been formulated within the horizon of a metaphysical and evolutionary conception of history. Today, it is precisely this philosophical horizon of history that has been lost. Consequently, an exact articulation of the philosophical theory of myth is no longer possible. This confusion is recorded and expressed in the common usage of the term 'myth'. On the one hand, the term continues to denote a form of knowledge that is no longer current, one that is often regarded as relatively primitive and which is certainly characterized vis-à-vis scientific knowledge as less objective, or at least less technologically useful. On the other hand, whether on account of the crisis undergone in philosophy by evolutionist metaphysics of history (along with the very ideal of scientific rationality), or for other less theoretical reasons more to do with political history, the conception of myth as primitive thought appears untenable. These confusions and contradictions are highlighted by a survey of the views that for the most part inform the use of the concept of myth today – views that I shall describe on the basis of certain ideal types rarely expressed in a pure form, either theoretically or practically, yet which are nonetheless to be found in our own cultural milieu. These predominant views may be arranged under three titles: archaism, cultural relativism and tempered irrationalism. All three, as we shall see shortly, are characterized by incoherencies and confusions deriving from a failure to resolve the problem of the philosophy of history that lies at the basis of every conception of myth. That is to say, they are born from a rejection of the metaphysics of history that underpinned the preceding theory of myth, but fall short theoretically themselves because they have still to elaborate a new philosophical conception of history; they have simply laid the problem aside.

The view I would describe as 'archaism' could also be called an 'apocalytpic view'. It concerns the widespread mistrust of Western techno-scientific culture as a way of life that violates and destroys our authentic relation to ourselves and to nature, and which is also inextricably bound to the system of capitalist exploitation and its imperialistic tendencies. The predilection of the early twentieth-century artistic avant-garde for African masks may be taken as a sign of art's often prophetic power regarding more general movements of culture and society. What for the historical artistic avant-garde was principally an interest in modes of representation of reality uncompromised by artistic languages inherited from the tradition – amply conjoined, at least in certain movements (surrealism, expressionism), with a thoroughgoing polemic against bourgeois culture – has become a common view today; to be sure, the liberal intelligentsia's bad conscience regarding the so-called third world is also evident in its stance towards myth. Besides, not only would the popularity enjoyed by structural anthropology as a cultural fashion be incomprehensible without this broadly political backdrop but, more generally, so would the fact that not only anthropological structuralism but structuralism in general appeared at the time of its greatest influence in popular culture to be a theoretical position of the 'left'. At the bottom of all this lay the idea that both the purely structural study of 'wild' myths and cultures and the consideration of man generally in non-historicist terms ('study men like ants,' said Lévi-Strauss in opposition to Sartre), were means of doing away with the Eurocentric ideology of progress, with all its imperialistic and colonial implications, in favour of a form of thought retrieving an 'authentic' relation between man and nature unmediated by scientific objectification and its links – exposed by the Frankfurt school, but also by the Lukács of *History and Class Consciousness* – with the capitalist organization of work. More recently, this critique and bad conscience with regard to imperialism and various forms of neo-colonialism have been joined by an ecological concern for the devastating consequences that science, technology, capitalist exploitation and the arms race are having on both the natural world and the physical nature of humanity.

With regard to myth, these factors all contribute towards what I call *archaism*. From this perspective, not only is myth not a primitive phase superseded by our own cultural history, it is in fact a more authentic form of knowledge, untouched by the devastating fanaticism for quantification and objectification characteristic of modern science, technology and capitalism. From the renewed contact with myth – whether the myths of 'other' cultures (studied by anthropologists amongst surviving communities of savages), or the ancient myths of our own tradition (the Greek myths, revisited by structuralist historians and philologists adopting the

Myth Rediscovered

methods and mentality of anthropologists) – there arises an expectation of a possible release from the distortions and contradictions of the present techno-scientific civilization. It seems to me that the popularity of Nietzsche and Heidegger in recent Continental European culture – despite equivocalities in interpretation that I will not go into here – is due in no small part to these considerations. The critique of techno-scientific society and the interest in archaic thought that one finds, in different forms, in both Nietzsche and Heidegger are taken as points of departure for an attempted recuperation of myth – even though neither Nietzsche nor Heidegger sanctions such an endeavour.

Yet, it would be hard to point to philosophical positions or cultural programmes that *explicitly* propose a return to mythical knowledge – with the exception of a faction within the movement in France and Italy that goes by the name of the 'new right', and that revives the anticapitalist polemic of Nazism and Fascism, combined with terms taken from the '68 movement. But, like the other two 'typic-ideal' views that I shall describe shortly, archaism does not give rise to actual doctrinal positions as such, for the reasons I have just mentioned. Whilst it is born out of the crisis in metaphysical historicism, it has no alternative to put forward and is therefore destined to remain theoretically mute, or at least not to be stated in precise theses. Even when archaism does not evolve into programmes for the restoration of traditional culture, with the 'right-wing' political positions these entail, it can still give rise to purely 'utopian' criticism of techno-scientific civilization and capitalism. Such is the case with much recent European liberal culture. Here, admittedly it makes no sense to try to restore the 'traditional' culture. In fact, it is actually politically dangerous and unacceptable. Yet mythical knowledge, uncompromised by the rationalism of the capitalist West, remains a benchmark for the rejection of modernity and its errors.

The second view that bears upon the presence of myth in our culture, and which makes it topical, is *cultural relativism*. According to this position, the principles and fundamental axioms that define rationality, truth-criteria and ethics, and which in general make possible the experience of a determinate historical humanity, or culture, are not objects of rational knowledge or demonstration; it is on them that the possibility of demonstrating anything depends. Thomas Kuhn's theory of paradigms, at least in its original form, is an expression of such a position that has gained great popularity in the epistemological debate of recent years.[4] Even hermeneutic theory going back to Heidegger is often taken to be a theory of this type, although there are good reasons for believing that it sees things differently itself. Not only does cultural relativism lack any idea of a univocal rationality in whose light certain forms of knowledge may be judged 'mythical'; in addition, and above all, the idea that the 'first principles' on which a specific cultural universe is constructed may not be objects or rational demonstrative knowledge leaves the way open for them to be considered objects of a mythical kind of knowledge. Even scientific rationality, which has for many centuries been of definitive value for European culture, is ultimately a myth, a shared belief on the basis of which our culture is organized. So (as Odo Marquard writes, for example[5]), the idea that the history of Western reason is the history of an exodus from myth, an *Entmythologisierung*, is a myth as well, an undemonstrated and indemonstrable article of faith.

In contrast to archaism, cultural relativism does not

accord mythical knowledge any (mythical) superiority over the scientific knowledge typical of modernity. In general, it simply denies any opposition between these two types of knowledge, since both of them are founded on presuppositions with the character of myth, that is, belief that is undemonstrated, yet experientially immediate. The fundamental beliefs of each cultural universe are not always called myths (cf. Marquard), but relativism's interest in myth is as lively as that of archaism. This does not reflect some attempt to rediscover in myth a more authentic knowledge. If studying the myths of other civilizations can teach us anything, it may be the correct method for knowing our own, for it too has a fundamentally mythical structure. As one can see clearly from Marquard's use of the term, myth amounts here to knowledge that is undemonstrated, experientially immediate, and its sense is still very much conditioned by its pure and simple opposition to the characteristics of scientific knowledge.

The third of the views on which the treatment of myth depends today is what I shall call *tempered irrationalism* or the theory of *limited rationality*. Here, the understanding of myth is somewhat more specific and moreover regains its links to the original etymological sense of the word. Myth, of course, means narration and in this form it is distinguished from scientific knowledge not by a simple inversion of the latter's characteristics, but by a positive feature of its own: narrative structure. In fact, the ensemble of cultural views that consider mythical knowledge, as essentially narrative, to be a form of thought better suited to certain regions of experience may be called a theory of limited rationality; this is not to contest or explicitly put into question the validity of positive-scientific knowledge in other fields of experience.

Myth Rediscovered

We can find examples of this position in at least three fields:

1 In psychoanalysis, interior life is generally taken to be structured according to narratives, both normally and when in therapy. Jungian psychoanalysis even considers there to be a necessary link between our interior life and certain fundamental 'stories' by which it is shaped, where these archetypal myths are neither abstract principles nor plays of forces etc., but precisely *stories*, and are, moreover, irreducible to structural models of which they would be merely symbols, allegories or applications (Hillman speaks of polytheism, I believe[6]).

2 The narrative model is increasingly relevant to the theory of historiography, for not only does it uncover the rhetorical models on which the constitution of historiography depends, but the irreducible *plurality* of these models reveals the basis for a negation of the unity of history. Insofar as this plurality no longer mirrors a reality-norm, it is increasingly difficult to distinguish it from a collection of myths.

3 In the sociology of the mass media, where the original application of the notion of myth to mass (revolutionary) movements proposed by Sorel has been replaced (most significantly, I believe) by analyses of the mythological character of images of the world distributed by cinema, television, literature and various consumer arts.

These various ways of treating the applicability of myth to different fields of experience may be described as tempered irrationalism or limited rationality, by virtue of their having a common presupposition that dates back to Plato,[7] namely that certain fields of experience are not susceptible to demonstrative reason or scientific method, and require instead another type of understanding that can only be described as mythical.

As I said at the beginning, these different views (inspiring different positions on myth, whilst themselves having mythical characteristics), are all born more or less directly out of a dissolution of metaphysical philosophies of history that they are unable to consummate (or consume). As a result, they display equivocalities and contradictions that render them theoretically unsatisfactory. To begin with, *archaism* does not pose itself the problem of history inasmuch as it fails to occupy a viable position with regard to the modern world other than, significantly, that of a right-wing restoration of 'traditional' culture. The significance of the traditionalism of the right, which is archaism's only visible political outlet, lies in the way that, by taking it to extremes, it exposes the theoretical weaknesses of simply reversing the myth of progress into a myth of origins, which *simply as such* would be more authentically human and worthy to serve either as ends of political revolution or, at least, as the benchmark for a critique of modernity.

To idealize the time of origins as perfect is as vacuous as idealizing the future (which is what the secular ideal of progress and development has done and continues to do). Moreover, we are in touch with the origins via the procession of events leading from them right down to ourselves. Archaism wishes simply to lay aside the problems this process presents; above all, if the origins have led to the very condition of unease, alienation etc., in which we find ourselves, why should we ever go back to them? It is problems of this kind, problems of the philosophy of history, that archaism lays aside without the discussion they deserve; yet they have in no way become less important with the decline of evolutionary metaphysics of history.

The same may be said of cultural relativism. Here, it is still more evident that the problem of history is neither posed nor resolved, but merely 'skipped'. Cultural relativism pays no attention to either (a) the actual context in which the thesis of the irreducible plurality of cultural worlds is put forward, or (b) the factual impossibility of isolating cultural worlds from one another, and not simply, as in (a), from our own universe, from ourselves as anthropologists and theoreticians of myth. The problem often faced by anthropologists working 'in the field' concerning the relation between themselves as representatives of a strong, often colonialist, culture and their indigenous informants is only one aspect of the wider hermeneutic problem cultural relativism leaves unasked. The study of 'other' cultures always takes place in a context that makes their supposed representation as separate objects impossible and contrived. Rather, they are involved in a dialogue, and once this is recognized it raises the problem of the common horizon within which it actually takes place, thereby undoing the separation relativism presupposes. This horizon is the problem of the philosophy of history and cannot be easily eliminated.

Ultimately, the theory of limited rationality, that is, the general idea that myth as knowledge in narrative form is a type of thought adequate to certain fields of experience (mass culture, interior life, historiography), also lays aside the problem of defining its own historical situation. It is unaware of its foundation on a tacit acceptance of the distinction between *Natur-* and *Geisteswissenschaften*; and this distinction has become increasingly problematic with the recognition that exact science is itself a social enterprise, and that the objectifying methods of the natural sciences are themselves, therefore, set entirely within the field of the socio-historical sciences.

In varying degrees and different ways – which could of course be investigated more fully – the three views regarding myth at large in today's culture disregard the question of their *own* historical contextualization far too hastily. They do not place themselves as theoretical positions. Archaism wants a return to origins and to mythical knowledge, without asking about the 'intermediary' period that separates us from that initial moment. Cultural relativism talks about separate and autonomous cultural universes, but does not say to which of these universes the theory of relativism belongs. Limited rationality has no clear account of how one is actually to distinguish between those fields reserved for mythical knowledge and those in which scientific rationality prevails. The metaphysics of history, whether idealist or positivist, has a response to each of these problems with its conception of history as a unilinear process of enlightenment and the emancipation of reason. The process of the emancipation of reason, however, has gone further than either idealism or positivism expected. Numerous peoples and cultures have taken to the world stage, and it has become impossible to believe that history is a unilinear process directed towards a *telos*. The realization of the universality of history has made universal history impossible. Consequently, the idea that the course of history could be thought of as enlightenment, as the liberation of reason from the shadows of mythical knowledge, has lost its legitimacy. Demythologization has itself come to be seen as a myth.[8]

But does the discovery of the mythical character of demythologization really legitimate the views regarding myth that we have described above? To demythologize the demythologization does not mean to restore the rights of myth, if only because amongst the myths we recognize as legitimate is that of reason and its progression. Demythologization, or the idea of history as the emancipation of reason, is not at all easy to exorcise. Nietzsche had already shown that the discovery of even the value of truth to be a belief founded on the exigencies of life, and thus an 'error', does not imply that the past errors are simply restored. To continue dreaming knowing that you are dreaming, as in the passage from the *Gay Science* quoted above, is by no means the same as purely and simply dreaming. And so it is with demythologization. If we wish to be faithful to our historical experience, we have to recognize that once demythologization has been exposed as a myth, our relation to myth does not return as naive as before, but remains marked by this experience. A theory of the presence of myth in today's culture must start afresh from this point. Nietzsche's words in the *Gay Science* are not simply a philosophical paradox. They are an expression of a destiny that belongs to our culture, a destiny that can also be denoted by another term, namely, *secularization*. The word conveys the two elements within the maxim from the *Gay Science*: to know one is dreaming and to go on dreaming. The secularization of the European spirit of the modern age does not consist solely in the exposure and demystification of the errors of religion, but also in the survival of these 'errors' in different, and in some sense degraded, forms. A secularized culture is not one that has simply left the religious elements of its tradition behind, but one that continues to live them as traces, as hidden and distorted models that are nonetheless profoundly present.

Myth Rediscovered

This is quite clear from reading Max Weber: modern capitalism is born not as the abandonment of the medieval Christian tradition, but as its 'transformed' application. Löwith's research on modern historicism makes the same point: the various metaphysics of history as far as Hegel, Marx, Comte are nothing but 'interpretations' of the Hebraic-Christian theology of history, thought outside their original theological frame. Less so in Löwith, but certainly in Weber, or even in Tönnies's community–society duality, the process whereby modernity (as industrial capitalism in Weber, as society no longer founded on organic bonds in Tönnies) cuts itself off from the original religious matrices appears to be an indivisible confluence of conquest and loss. Modernization does not come about as tradition is abandoned, but as it is interpreted almost ironically, 'distorted' (Heidegger, in a not unrelated fashion, talks of *Verwindung*[9]) in such a way that it is conserved, but also in part emptied. Alongside these elements of secularization, one could place both Norbert Elias's theory of European civilization,[10] and Girard's theories on the sacred as violence and Christianity as a process of desacralization.[11] In Elias, the process of modern civilization develops when the power and exercise of force is concentrated in the sovereign, in the initially absolute and then constitutional State. Accordingly, the collective psychology undergoes a radical transformation: singular individuals in all social classes interiorize the 'good manners' of members of the court, who were the first to renounce force in the sovereign's favour; the passions are no longer strong and open as in past ages; existence loses vivacity and colour, but gains security and formalization. Here too, progress is accompanied by a lessening intensity of experience, a kind of evacuation or dilution. As for

Myth Rediscovered

Girard, his discourse concerns human civilization in general, whose trajectory, in his opinion, runs from the birth of the sacred – which discharges the violence of all against all by focusing it on the sacrificial victim, yet thereby allows it to survive as the basis of institutions – up to its demystification by the Old Testament and Jesus. It is Jesus who shows the sacred to be violence, and so opens the way to a new human history that, in opposition to Girard's terminology and intentions, we can clearly deem secularized.

Modern European culture is thus linked to its own religious past not only by a relation of overcoming and emancipation, but also, and inseparably, by a relation to conservation–distortion–evacuation: progress is in a sense nostalgic by nature, as the classicism and romanticism of recent centuries have taught us. But the significance of this nostalgia only becomes apparent once the experience of demythologization is taken to its extreme. When demythologization itself is revealed as myth, myth regains legitimacy, but only within the frame of a generally 'weakened' experience of truth. The presence of myth in our culture does not represent an alternative or opposing movement to modernization, but is rather its natural outcome, its destination, at least thus far. The demythologization of demythologization, moreover, may be taken as the true moment of transition from the modern to the postmodern. This transition occurs in its most philosophically explicit form in Nietzsche. After him, after radical demythologization, the experience of truth simply can no longer be the same as before; there is no longer apodictic evidence, in which thinkers of the metaphysical age sought a *fundamentum absolutum et iconcussum*. If the postmodern subject looks into itself in search of a primary certainty, in place of the security of the

Myth Rediscovered

Cartesian *cogito*, it finds the intermittencies of the Proustian heart, stories from the media, *mythologies* evinced by psychoanalysis.

It is this experience (modern or postmodern) that the 'return' of myth in our culture and language tries to capture, rather than a renaissance of myth as knowledge untainted by modernization and rationalization. Only in this sense does the 'return of myth', if and insofar as it takes place, seem to point towards an overcoming of the opposition between rationalism and irrationalism – an overcoming, however, that reopens the problem of a renewed philosophical consideration of history.

NOTES

1. C. Lévi-Strauss, *Structural Anthropology* (1958) (Penguin Books, Harmondsworth, 1968), p. 209.
2. E.g. the final chapter of C. Lévi-Strauss, *The Naked Man* (*Introduction to a Science of Mythology*, vol. 4; 1971) (Cape, London, 1981), and the opening section of *The Raw and the Cooked* (*Introduction to the Science of Mythology*, vol. 1; 1964) (Cape, London, 1970).
3. E. Cassirer, *Philosophy of Symbolic Forms* vol. 2 (1923), tr. R. Manheim (Yale University Press, New Haven, Conn., 1966), p. 1.
4. T. Kuhn, *The Structure of Scientific Revolutions* (1962) (University of Chicago Press, 1970).
5. O. Marquard, *Farewell to Matters of Principle: Philosophical Studies* (1981) tr. R. M. Wallace (Oxford University Press, New York, 1989).
6. D. L. Miller and J. Hillman, *New Polytheism: Rebirth of the Gods and Goddesses* (New York, 1974).
7. E.g. Plato, *Timaeus* 19d.
8. Marquard, *Farewell to Matters of Principle*, and the whole of the essay 'Lob des Polytheismus' (In praise of polytheism).

9 Regarding the notion of *Verwindung* in Heidegger and its interpretation in the sense intended here, cf. ch. 10 of my *End of Modernity* (1985), tr. J. Snyder (Polity Press, Cambridge, 1988).
10 Esp. N. Elias, *Power and Civility* (1937), tr. E. Jephcott, (Pantheon, New York, 1982).
11 R. Girard, *Violence and the Sacred* (1972), tr. P. Gregory (Athlone Press, London, 1988); and esp. R. Girard, *Things Hidden since the Foundation of the World* (1978), tr. P. Gregory (Athlone Press, London, 1987).

4

Art and Oscillation

As in the whole of modernity,[1] it may be that the distinctive character of existence, or in Heidegger's terms the 'meaning of being' in our epoch, appears first and most clearly in aesthetic experience. It therefore deserves special attention, if we wish to understand what is to become not only of art in late modernity, but more generally of being.

The problem of art in a society of generalized communication was decisively addressed by Walter Benjamin in his 1936 essay 'The work of art in the age of mechanical reproduction'[2] – a text that is still relevant today and one we should keep going back to, for in my view it has never been properly assimilated and 'digested', so to speak, by subsequent research in aesthetics. In fact, it has generally been understood as nothing more than a straightforward sociological account of the new conditions under which contemporary art operates. As such, it has been used either as an instrument of polemic against the art market or as the theoretical basis for a reflection on all artistic phenomena located outside the traditional institutions of art (outside the theatre, as in the 'happening' [in English in the original – Trans.];

Art and Oscillation

outside the museum and the gallery, as in various forms of performance art, landscape art, etc.). Alternatively, it has been dismissed as expressing an illusion, namely that the technical reproduction of art might offer a positive opportunity for its rejuvenation, whereas in reality, as Adorno maintained, the standardized civilization he experienced in America is a long way from realizing Benjamin's utopia, and reflects instead the total uniformity all art acquires through the manipulation of consensus by the mass media. Yet these various readings of Benjamin's essay seem broadly inadequate. We need to go back to this essay and reflect on its central intuition, namely, the idea that the new conditions of artistic production and appreciation that obtain in the society of mass media substantially modify the essence of art, its *Wesen* (a term we shall use in the Heideggerian sense: not the eternal nature of art, but its way of *giving itself* in the present epoch).

Neither Adorno, in his radical critique of reproduction, nor any of the sociological interpretations (which even go so far as to hope, like Marcuse, for an aesthetic reconciliation of existence), have added anything new, or even of the same stature, to Benjamin's remarks on this change of essence. When Adorno denies that art can (or should) actually lose the *aura* that isolates the work from the everyday, he defends the critical power of the work with respect to existing reality, whilst also adopting and maintaining the traditional conception of art as a place of harmony and perfection that runs throughout Western metaphysics from Aristotle to Hegel. That the harmony is utopian and belongs within the realm of appearance, as Adorno underlines in an opportune deployment of Kant against Hegel, does not mean a true change in essence, however, but only its location in an indefinite future, where its role remains that of a regulative ideal. This point warrants our attention, even at a time of renewed interest in Adorno's aesthetics and the thought of Ernst Bloch, above all in France (a little later than in other cultural circles, such as Italy).

Benjamin's comments open the way for a reflection on the new *Wesen* of art in late-industrial society that overcomes the traditional metaphysical definition of art as a place of harmony, correspondence between inside and outside, catharsis. These points can be developed satisfactorily on the basis of an analogy that looks paradoxical at first sight, and which to my knowledge has still not been remarked upon. Benjamin's essay was written in 1936, the same year another key text for contemporary aesthetics was born, namely, Heidegger's essay 'Der Ursprung des Kunstwerkes' (The origin of the work of art).[3] This is the text in which Heidegger elaborates his central notion of the work of art as the 'setting-into-work of truth' arising in the strife between the work's two constitutive elements: the setting up of the world and the setting forth of the earth. Heidegger defines the effect on the observer of such a work by the term *Stoss* – literally, a blow. Although the basis and meaning of the theory we find in Benjamin's essay appear to be quite different, it describes the effect of cinema, as the art-form most characteristic of the age of technical reproduction, precisely in terms of *shock*. The view I wish to put forward is that by developing the analogy between Heidegger's *Stoss* and Benjamin's *shock*, we shall be able to assemble the essential features of a new 'essence' of art in late-industrial society, features that have eluded even the most acute and radical reflections on contemporary aesthetics, including those of Adorno.

Technical reproduction seems to work in exactly the

opposite sense to *shock*. In the age of reproduction, both the great art of the past and new media products reproducible from their inception, such as cinema, tend to become common consumer objects and consequently less and less well defined against the background of intensified communication. This growing psychological dullness could be put down to symbols being transmitted and multiplied too quickly and 'wearing themselves out'. But this is not the only way that the technical means of reproduction tend to level out works. No matter how perfect, such means end up picking out and accentuating those characteristics of the work most 'visible' to them, or else forcing the work within limits set by the means themselves. Adorno, for example, objected strongly to the distortions of musical tempi that can result from pieces being squeezed onto record.

Of course, this conflict between the work's 'being in itself' and its adaptation to the means of reproduction only arises if – like Adorno – one still distinguishes between a work's ideal 'use value' and its alienated and degenerate 'exchange' value (linked to market conditions, fashions etc.). As we know, in his 1936 essay Benjamin on the contrary welcomed as a decisive and positive step the change brought about by technical reproduction, whereby the 'cult' value of a work gave way entirely to its 'exhibition' value. This amounted to saying that the work has no 'use value' apart from its exchange value, or that its entire aesthetic significance is inseparable from the history of its *Wirkung*, of its fate, appreciation and interpretation in culture and society. (This, incidentally, is not the same as advocating the purely hermeneutic nihilism expressed in the words of Valéry, 'mes vers ont le sens qu'on leur prête'; individual interpretations are not weighed up in a vacuum, but are linked to all other interpretations, to

Art and Oscillation

the global *Wirkungsgeschichte,* or 'effective history' of the work in a way that is not only historico-factual, but also normative.[4])

But the problem of the relation between cult value – or 'aural' value, in Benjamin's sense – and exhibition value can only be resolved if the implications of the theory of *shock* are followed through to the end. As long as the appreciation of the work of art is thought of in terms of the appreciation of formal perfection and the experience of satisfaction at this perfection, it will be impossible to accept that, as we have said, use value dissolves into exchange value, or that cult value gives way to exhibition value.

In Benjamin's essay, the shock-effect is presented as characteristic of the cinema, which in this respect had been anticipated by Dada. The Dadaist work of art is actually conceived as a projectile launched at the spectator, at his every security, sensory expectation and perceptual habit. The cinema too is made up of projectiles, of projections: as soon as an image is formed, it is replaced by another to which the spectator's eye and mind must readapt. In a note to the essay, Benjamin explicitly compares the perceptual competence required when watching a film with that of a pedestrian (or, we might add, a driver) in the midst of traffic in a big modern city. 'Film', writes Benjamin 'is the art that is in keeping with the increased threat to life which modern man has to face.'[5] It is as if we read here, albeit curiously demythologized and scaled down to everyday life (the risks of traffic), what Heidegger thematizes in his essay 'The origin of the work of art' with the notion of *Stoss*. In a sense distinct from Benjamin's, yet perhaps profoundly close to it, Heidegger too takes the experience of the *shock* of art to be concerned with death – not so much with the risk of

Art and Oscillation

being run over by a bus, as with death as a possibility that is constitutive of existence. In the experience of art, according to Heidegger, it is the very fact of the work's being-there rather than not that gives rise to the *Stoss*.[6] The fact of a thing's being-there, its *Dass*, as readers of *Being and Time* will recall,[7] is also at the root of the existential experience of anxiety. In section 40 of *Being and Time* anxiety is described as the mood of *Dasein* (human being) when confronted with the naked fact of its being thrown into the world. Whilst single things belong to the world insofar as they are inserted in a referential totality of significance (each thing is referred to others, as effect, cause, instrument, sign, etc.), the world as such and as a whole does not refer and thus has no significance. Anxiety is a mark of this insignificance, the utter gratuitousness of the fact that the world is. The experience of anxiety is an experience of 'uncanniness' (of *Un-heimlichkeit*, or *Un-zu-Haus-sein*).[8] The analogy of the *Stoss* of art with this experience of anxiety may be appreciated if one recalls that the work of art does not allow itself to be drawn back into a pre-established network of significance, at least insofar as it cannot be deduced as a logical consequence. Moreover, it does not simply slot into the world as it is, but purports to shed new light upon it. As Heidegger describes it, the encounter with the work of art is like an encounter with someone whose view of the world is a challenge to our own interpretation. It is above all in this sense that one must understand the Heideggerian thesis according to which the work of art *founds* a world by presenting itself as a new historical event or 'opening' of Being. Although the *Stoss* seems to be described in more 'positive' terms than anxiety in *Being and Time*, which always concerns *Stimmungen* like fear, preoccupation, etc., its meaning is essentially the same: that of

Art and Oscillation

suspending the familiarity of the world, of stimulating a preoccupied wonder at the fact, in itself insignificant (strictly speaking, since it refers to nothing, or refers to the nothing), that the world is there.

To what extent is this notion of *Stoss* actually related, other than terminologically, to the *shock* spoken of by Benjamin in connection with the media of reproduction? Heidegger seems to link the *Stoss* of the work of art to its 'setting-into-work of truth', that is, to its being a new ontologico-epochal opening. In this sense, one should speak of *Stoss* only in reference to the great works that present themselves as decisive points in a culture's history, or at least in the experience of individuals: the Bible, the Greek tragedies, Dante, Shakespeare, and so on. Benjamin's *shock* seems instead to be something much simpler and more familiar, such as the rapid succession of projected images whose demands on a viewer are analogous to those made on a driver in city traffic. Yet the two conceptions, Heidegger's and Benjamin's, have at least one feature in common: their insistence on disorientation. In each case, aesthetic experience appears to be an experience of estrangement, which then requires recomposition and readjustment. However, the aim of this is not to reach a final recomposed state. Instead, aesthetic experience is *directed towards keeping the disorientation alive*. For Benjamin, given his chosen example of the cinema, it is all too clear that we cannot regard the experience of film as fulfilled when it is reduced to a single still frame. For Heidegger, the experience of disorientation that belongs to art is in opposition to the familiarity of the object of use, in which the enigmatic character of the *Dass* (the 'that-it-is') dissolves in usability. One cannot attribute to Heidegger the view that the experience of aesthetic disorientation 'concludes' in a recuperation of familiarity

Art and Oscillation

and obviousness, almost as though it were ultimately the destiny of the art-work to transform itself into a simple object of use. The state of disorientation, for both Heidegger and Benjamin, is constitutive and not provisional. This is precisely what is most radically new about these aesthetic positions compared with both traditional reflections on the beautiful and the survival of this tradition in the aesthetic theories of this century. From the Aristotelian doctrine of catharsis to the free play of the Kantian faculties, to the beautiful as the perfect correspondence of inside and outside in Hegel, aesthetic experience seems always to have been described in terms of *Geborgenheit* – security, 'orientation' or 'reorientation'.

The novel element in the positions of Heidegger and Benjamin, by virtue of which they break with every conception of aesthetic experience given in terms of *Geborgenheit*, may be identified via the notion of oscillation. This calls for a shift in emphasis with respect to the usual interpretation of Heidegger's aesthetics. For if the 'founding' role art plays in relation to the world is overstated, one ends up with a view heavily laden with romanticism. To be sure, this refrain too is there in Heidegger: 'poets alone ordain what abides', to cite the line he often recalls from Hölderlin, meaning that the decisive turns of language, which is the 'house of Being', the place where the fundamental coordinates of every possible experience of the world are delineated, occur in poetry.

Yet Heidegger's concern, and this comes to light in many passages of the 1936 essay and in his readings of the poets, is not to give a positive definition of the world that poetry opens and founds, but rather to determine the significance of the 'unfounding'[9] which is always an inseparable part of poetry. Foundation and

Art and Oscillation

unfounding are the meaning of the two features Heidegger identifies as constitutive of the work of art, namely, the setting up (*Auf-stellung*) of the world and the setting forth (*Her-stellung*) of the 'earth'. The world is set up as the system of significations it inaugurates; the earth is set forth by the work insofar as it is put forward, shown, as the obscure and thematically inexhaustible depths in which the world of the work is rooted. If, as we have seen, disorientation is essential to aesthetic experience, and not merely provisional, it owes far more to earth than to world. Only because the world of significance unfolded in the work seems to be obscurely rooted (hence not logically 'founded') in the earth, can the effect of the work be one of disorientation. Earth is not world. It is not a system of signifying connections: it is other, the nothing, general gratuitousness and insignificance. The work is a foundation only insofar as it produces an ongoing disorientation that can never be recuperated in a final *Geborgenheit*. The work of art is never serene, never 'beautiful' in the sense of a perfect harmony between inside and outside, essence and existence, etc. It may have something of Aristotelian catharsis about it, but only if catharsis is understood as an exercise in finitude, a recognition of the insuperable terrestrial limits of human existence; not perfect purification, but rather *phronesis*. Thus, it is not so much in terms of founding as of unfounding that an analogy may be drawn between the Heideggerian *Stoss* and the shock to which Benjamin refers. The analogy will elude us and seem absurd if we contrast the apparent insignificance of Benjamin's shock with too inflated a view of the work of art as an inauguration and foundation of historico-cultural worlds. But to read Heidegger's theory in this way is still to interpret it in a metaphysical, or in Heidegger's terms ontical, form, such that the *Stoss* would depend on the weight and distinctive proportions of the new world inaugurated and founded by the work. To interpret and appreciate the work would mean to establish oneself in this world and its new manner of signifying. It becomes clear, however, that, as with anxiety, what interests Heidegger about the *Stoss* is its disorientating effect with regard to any world whatsoever – whether the given world or that set out in positive terms by the work.

'Film', writes Benjamin, 'is the art that is in keeping with the increased threat to life.' But in the context of his essay as a whole, it is also the art that realizes the late-modern essence of every art, and in whose light alone aesthetic experience as such – even of art-works from the past – is now possible. This experience can no longer be characterized as a king of *Geborgenheit*, a security and harmony. Rather, it is essentially precarious, linked not only to the risk of accident run by the pedestrian, but to the precarious structure of existence in general. The *shock* characteristic of new forms of reproducible art is simply the expression in our own world of Heidegger's *Stoss*, the essential oscillation and disorientation constitutive of the experience of art.

In Benjamin's essay, one perceives a generally positive evaluation of technology. For him, the end of the cult and aural value of the work of art represents a clear opportunity of liberating ourselves from the art of superstition and alienation, and ultimately from the chains of metaphysics. In contrast, Heidegger seems to be a harsh judge of modern existence, not least because the increasingly banal character of language in the society of generalized communication destroys the very possibility of the work existing *qua* work, flattening it into insignificance. Yet it is hard to present Heidegger as a theoretician of the work of art as a cult item – as if he saw the aesthetic value of the work in the *hic et nunc* of its presence *qua* successful and perfect form, produced by the artist as a creative genius. These are all categories that, although essential to the cult conception of the work of art, are radically foreign to Heidegger, for whom the work is the 'setting-into-work of truth' precisely insofar as it is always more than art, more than an accomplished and perfect form, more than the result of mastery or a creative act. The work functions as an opening of the truth because it is an 'event' (*Ereignis*) of being, which has its essence as event in being overturned and 'expropriated' in the 'mirror-play of the world' (as Heidegger says in his essay 'The thing'[10]).

However, it is more important here to pursue the other problem, namely Heidegger's approach to human existence in the technical world. In clarifying this problem we may uncover something of importance regarding the disorientation and oscillation intrinsic to aesthetic experience in late modernity, and this may help us to develop those elements in Benjamin's proposals that have so far remained implicit. (In passing, we might note that both Heidegger and Benjamin draw on Georg Simmel's description of human existence in the modern metropolis.[11] If we go back to the passages of *Identity and Difference* and *The Question Concerning Technology* where Heidegger illustrates his notion of *Ge-stell*,[12] we find that he uses this term, roughly translatable as 'enframing', to characterize the whole apparatus of modern technology. This may in general be thought as a *Stellen*, a 'setting up': man sets up things as objects of his manipulation, but he is in turn forever called upon to meet new demands, such that *Ge-stell* is a kind of continual and frantic reciprocal provocation on the part of man and being. But the essence of modern technology defined in this way is not only the highest point of the metaphysical oblivion of being. For Heidegger, *Ge-stell* is also 'a first, oppressing flash of *Ereignis*',[13] that is of the event of being, beyond the metaphysical oblivion of being.[14] Precisely in the *Ge-stell*, that is, in the society of technology and total manipulation, Heidegger sees an opportunity of overcoming the oblivion and metaphysical alienation in which Western man has lived until now. The *Ge-stell* can offer such an opportunity because it is defined in almost identical terms to those used by Benjamin in speaking of *shock*.

In fact, in the *Ge-stell*, Heidegger writes: 'Our whole human existence everywhere sees itself challenged – now playfully and now urgently, now breathlessly and now ponderously – to devote itself to the planning and calculating of everything.'[15] The provocation to which the existence of modern man is subject is analogous to the condition of Benjamin's pedestrian, for whom art can only be *shock*, continual disorientation and ultimately an exercise in mortality. The opportunity of overcoming metaphysics offered by the *Ge-stell* is linked to the fact that in it man and being lose 'those qualities with which metaphysics has endowed them'.[16] Nature is no longer the place of necessary law and the 'positive sciences', whilst the human world – itself rigorously subjected to technologies of manipulation – is no longer the complementary and diametrically opposed realm of freedom, the field of the 'human sciences'. Accordingly, in this reshuffle, as the theatre of metaphysics with its well-defined roles wanes, so an opportunity for a new advent of being dawns.

Is the aesthetic terminology at our disposal, the concepts that recur again and again in different forms whenever we talk of art (of its production or apprecia-

Art and Oscillation

tion), adequate for thinking aesthetic experience as disorientation, oscillation, unfounding and shock? An indication to the contrary may be seen in the fact that aesthetic theory has yet to do justice to the mass media and the possibilities they offer. It is as if it were always a matter of 'saving' some essence of art (creativity, originality, appreciation of form, harmony, etc.) from the menace the new existential state of mass society presents not only to art, it is said, but also to the very essence of man. Reproducibility is thought to be irreconcilable with the seemingly indispensable demands for creativity in art. This is due only in part to the fact that the rapid diffusion of information tends to render every message immediately banal (indeed, in order to keep the media satisfied, such messages are banal from birth). Above all, it is because the reaction to this depletion of symbols is the invention of 'novelties' that, like those of fashion, have none of the radicality seemingly necessary to the work of art. They are presented as superficial games; indeed, everything sent out by the mass media is imbued with a strange air of fragility and superficiality. This clearly clashes with the preconceptions of an aesthetic that draws its inspiration more or less explicitly from the ideal of the art work as a *momentum aere perennius*, and of the deep and authentic involvement of the subject in aesthetic experience, either as creator or as spectator. A stability and permanence in the work, a depth and authenticity in the aesthetic experience of creation and appreciation are things we can no longer expect from late-modern aesthetic experience, dominated as it is by the power (and impotence) of the media. In opposition to the nostalgia for eternity (in the work) and authenticity (in experience), it must be clearly recognized that *shock* is all that remains of the creativity of art in the age of

Art and Oscillation

generalized communication. And *shock* is defined by the two characteristics we have singled out with the help of Benjamin and Heidegger: fundamentally, it is nothing but metropolitan man's nervous and intellectual inconstancy and hypersensitivity. The focal point for art corresponding to this excitability and hypersensitivity is no longer the *work*, but *experience*, where this is thought of in terms of a minimal and continual variation (exemplified by watching film). These issues have often been treated by nineteenth- and twentieth-century aesthetic theory, though their consequences have never been fully worked out: for example, Heidegger draws our attention to them – polemically – in Nietzsche's theory of art.

The second feature constitutive of *shock* as the sole remnant of creativity in late-modern art is what Heidegger thinks via the notion of *Stoss*, namely the disorientation and oscillation connected with anxiety and the experience of mortality. The phenomenon Benjamin describes as shock, then, does not concern only the conditions of perception, and nor is it simply to be entrusted to the sociology of art. Rather, it is the manner of the work of art's actualization as conflict between world and earth. *Shock–Stoss* is the *Wesen*, the essence, of art in the two senses this expression has in Heidegger's terminology. It is the way in which aesthetic experience presents itself in late modernity, and it is also that which appears to be essential for art *tout court*; that is, its occurrence as the nexus of foundation and unfounding in the form of oscillation and disorientation – and ultimately as the task of mortality.

Is this to offer too hasty an apology for mass culture, as though it were redeemed of all the alienating characteristics so tellingly identified by Adorno and critical sociology? The equivocality of this sociology in our own day seems to arise from a failure to distinguish between the conditions of political alienation proper to society as total organization and the novel elements implicit in late-modern existence. As a result of this equivocality, the perversity of standardization and total organization has often been condemned in the name of humanistic values whose critical significance was due entirely to their being anachronistic. In fact, such values pre-date the metaphysics whose outcome, as Heidegger saw very clearly, has been the total organization of society. Perhaps we have now reached the stage where we can recognize that the superficiality and fragility of aesthetic experience in late-modern society do not necessarily have to be signs and symptoms of alienation linked to the dehumanizing aspects of standardization.

Contrary to what critical sociology has long believed (with good reason, unfortunately), standardization, uniformity, the manipulation of consensus and the errors of totalitarianism *are not* the only possible outcome of the advent of generalized communication, the mass media and reproduction. Alongside these possibilities – which are objects of political choice – there opens an alternative possible outcome. The advent of the media enhances the inconstancy and superficiality of experience. In so doing, it runs counter to the generalization of domination, insofar as it allows a kind of 'weakening' of the very notion of reality, and thus a weakening of its persuasive force. The society of the spectacle spoken of by the situationists is not simply a society of appearance manipulated by power: it is also the society in which reality presents itself as softer and more fluid, and in which experience can again acquire the characteristics of oscillation, disorientation and play.

The ambiguity many contemporary theories take to

be characteristic of aesthetic experience is not provisional: it is not a matter of mastering language in general more completely – as subjects – by the freer and less automated use of language found in poetry. This would merely be to use poetic ambiguity as a means towards the fuller appropriation of language by the subject. As such, it would be a matter of an intentional disorientation aiming at an ultimate reorientation still hostage, if not to the category of 'work', then certainly to the corresponding category of 'subject'. On the contrary, art is constituted as much by the experience of ambiguity as it is by oscillation and disorientation. In the world of generalized communication, these are the only ways that art can (not *still*, but perhaps *finally*) take the form of creativity and freedom.

NOTES

1 Cf. ch. 6 of my *End of Modernity* (1985), tr. J. Snyder, (Polity Press, Cambridge, 1988).
2 Published in English in W. Benjamin, *Illuminations*, tr. H. Zohn, ed. H. Arendt (Jonathan Cape, London 1982).
3 M. Heidegger, 'The origin of the work of art', in *Poetry Language Thought*, tr. A. Hofstadter (Harper & Row, New York, 1971).
4 This is one of the central terms of contemporary hermeneutic debate. Cf. H. G. Gadamer, *Truth and Method* (1960) (London, Sheed & Ward, 1975), pp. 305ff.
5 W. Benjamin, 'The work of art . . .', in *Illuminations*, p. 252, n. 19.
6 Heidegger, *Poetry Language Thought*, pp. 65–6.
7 M. Heidegger, *Being and Time* (1927), tr. J. Macquarrie and E. Robinson (Basil Blackwell, Oxford, 1980).
8 Ibid., pp. 233–4.
9 ['sfondamento'. In Italian, the addition of an 's' to an existing word often reverses the meaning of that word:

e.g. *contento* (happy) – *scontento* (unhappy), *fondare* (to found) – *sfondare* (to break through or knock the bottom (*fondo*) out of something). In general, then, the term *sfondamento* means 'breaking'. However, it could also be taken as 'non-foundation', the contrary of *fondamento*. This sense is clearly implicit in Vattimo's use of the term. In addition, Vattimo plays on the word's connection with *sfondo*, which generally means 'background' (but which could also be read as the contrary of *fondo*, which means bottom, end or base), thereby suggesting a further sense of 'setting a thing in place against a background'. Vattimo mentions this sense explicitly on p. 73 – Trans.]

10 The essay is included in Heidegger, *Poetry Language Thought*.
11 Cf. Georg Simmel's essay 'Metropolis and mental life' (1902), in *Second Year Course in the Study of Contemporary Society* (Chicago, Univ. Chicago Bookstore, 1936), pp. 221–38.
12 M. Heidegger, *Identity and Difference* (1957), tr. J. Stambaugh (Harper & Row, New York, 1969); *The Question Concerning Technology and Other Essays*, tr. W. Lovitt (Harper & Row, New York, 1977).
13 Heidegger, *Identity and Difference*, p. 38.
14 There is a further discussion of the concept of the oblivion of being proper to metaphysics, and of other terms from Heidegger's philosophy, in my *Introduction to Heidegger* (Laterza, Rome/Bari, 1982).
15 Heidegger, *Identity and Difference*, pp. 34–5.
16 Ibid., p. 37.

5

From Utopia to Heterotopia

The most radical transformation in the relation between art and everyday life to have occurred since the sixties may be described as a transition from *utopia* to *heterotopia*. The sixties (certainly '68 above all, but the struggles of that year were simply the culmination of a movement that had begun shortly after the war) saw a broad range of views concerned with an aesthetic rehabilitation of existence, all of which more or less explicitly denied art its 'special' status as the 'Sunday of life', as Hegel put it. The most explicit and radical form of utopia is obviously to be found in Marxism, but it also has a bourgeois form in the ideology of *design*, which has been widely influential, most especially via the popularity of Dewey in European philosophy and critique in the fifties.[1] Like the Marxist theoreticians and critics (from Lukács to Marcuse and the heads of the Frankfurt school), Dewey too is of Hegelian descent. In his view, the experience of the beautiful is linked to the perception of a *fulfilment* that could not survive a separation from the concreteness of everyday life. For if there is such a thing as art in the narrow sense, it points

From Utopia to Heterotopia

to a more general sensation of harmony rooted in our use of objects and the achievement of a satisfactory balance between individual and environment. As for the various forms of Marxism, they share the view that the independence of art and the specificity of aesthetic experience are features of the division of labour, which is to be abolished by revolution, or at least by a transformation of society in which the whole essence of humanity is reappropriated by the people as a whole. In Lukács, this view functions primarily at the level of critical methodology (realism does not simply mirror things as they are, but represents the age and its conflicts with implicit reference to emancipation and reappropriation). In Adorno,[2] the *promesse de bonheur* constitutive of art is presented in predominantly negative terms as an exposure of the discordance of the existent – along with the corresponding 'revolutionary' revaluation of the historical avant-garde, which Lukácsian realism regarded instead as symptomatic of pure decadence. But it is in Marcuse's dream of an aesthetic (sensory and sensuous) rehabilitation of existence as a whole that the full implications of the utopian revaluation of the avant-garde are set out most clearly.[3] If, from the Marxist point of view, Adorno paved the way towards a positive attitude to movements of the avant-garde, particularly as formal revolutions in the languages of the various arts (Schoenberg's twelve-note scale, Beckett's silence), Marcuse's utopia is a 'synthesis' of other important aspects of the avant-garde, such as the general transformation of relations between aesthetic experience and everyday existence instigated by surrealism and situationism. In the background of all this stand some of the great names of critical Marxism – Benjamin for Adorno, Bloch for Marcuse, as well as figures such as Henri Lefebvre,[4] more closely linked to the avant-garde and its continuation right up to the early fifties, in situationism, for example.

The relative distance that now separates us from those years has seemingly attenuated the not insignificant differences between, for example, the ideology of *design* (the dream of an aesthetic rehabilitation of everydayness by an elevation of the forms of objects and the appearance of our surroundings) and the revolutionary approach of the various Marxisms. Amidst these differing points of view, the aim has always been to achieve a comprehensive fusion of aesthetic and existential meaning that could rightfully call itself a utopia. Utopia was, according to Ernst Bloch's famous 1918 work,[5] the meaning of the artistic avant-garde of the early twentieth century. Although these movements were in many respects superseded by the ideology of *design* (historically, this was the case with the Bauhaus), over the course of a long development (from their rejection by Lukács, to Adorno and finally Marcuse) they became bound up with revolutionary Marxism (and at the level of the masses this bond is one of the meanings, or *the* meaning, of '68).

This grand utopia was to be an aesthetic unification of experience, and to bring together diverse political and theoretical stances, inclining them away from what Nietzsche called 'the art of the work of art' towards either *design* or the revolutionary rehabilitation of existence as a whole. Yet little of this seems to remain now. As far as I am aware, it is rare these days for critique to pose explicitly the question of the meaning of art as such, along with that of the meaning and value of the work.

What Adorno regarded as the essence of the avant-garde, namely its ability to place the very essence of art in question with a single work, no longer seems to be the case today. It is as if the 'system of spirit', with all its distinctions and specialisms, were entirely back in place. Paradoxically, even Habermas's work, which presents itself as a defence of the permanent value of the modern programme of emancipation, sees no problem in taking its bearings from the Kantian distinction between different kinds of social action – teleological, rule-governed, expressive and dramatic, somehow reserving the aesthetic sphere for the last of these.[6] Communicative action, which for Habermas is at the pinnacle of this typology, does not really put the distinction between the other three in question, indeed it serves as a transcendental principle on guard against any undue infringements (primarily by any of the interests expressed in the three forms of action to the detriment of communication, but probably also by any of the three types of activity upon each other). However, without discussing Habermas's *Theory of Communicative Action* in detail, I wish only to show that it contains an example of a certain theoretical restoration of the independence and specialization of the aesthetic realm that, according to a tradition of thought rooted deeply in modernity, is here drawn back to expressivity.

Habermas's redeployment of the Kantian tripartite structure of reason is only a symptom of the general situation to which I wish to refer, and is not cited as a necessarily 'negative' phenomenon, nor as a theoretical and practical regression to be criticized (although, as I hope will become clear, I do not share Habermas's position and his strenuous defence of the currency of the modern). This aspect of Habermas's theory expresses the decline of utopia and the return to an untroubled acceptance of the independence of the aesthetic. Yet this is not the only, nor even the primary, way that the relation between art and everyday life has been changing in recent years. Habermas's revival of Kantian aesthetics could also be taken as evidence that his defence of the Enlightenment and modernity implies a specific deafness towards many phenomena concerned with the standardization of 'aesthetic' culture that Habermas does not 'wish' to see and whose significance he is reluctant to recognize. Art's retreat within its own borders, after the utopia of the sixties, is only one aspect of the situation that interests us, and that Habermas – as far as aesthetics is concerned – seems to single out in accordance with certain of his theoretical prejudices (such as his rejection of postmodernism).

The utopia of the sixties is in some sense coming to fruition beneath our very eyes, albeit in a distorted and transformed fashion. If, on the one hand, art in the traditional sense of the work of art reverts to order, on the other, the site of aesthetic experience in society is shifting: not simply towards the generalization of design and a universal social hygiene with regard to forms, nor even as a Marcusian aesthetico-revolutionary rehabilitation of existence, but rather in the sense of an unfolding of the capacity of the aesthetic product – nowise the work of art – to 'make world', to create community. From this point of view, the most theoretically appropriate and faithful interpretation of aesthetic experience manifest in recent years is perhaps that put forward by Gadamerian hermeneutic ontology. For Gadamer, as we know, the experience of beauty is characterized by mutual recognition within a community of those who appreciate similar natural objects and artworks of beauty.[7] Judgement is reflexive, in Kantian terminology, not only because it refers to the state of the subject instead of the object, but also because it refers to the subject as a member of a community (to some extent, this is already apparent in certain pages of the

Critique of Judgement). The experience of the beautiful, then, more fundamentally than the experience of a structure we simply find pleasing (yet on the basis of what criteria?), is the experience of belonging to a community. It is easy to see how and why such a conception of the aesthetic can present itself so persuasively today. For mass culture has magnified this aspect of the aesthetic's nature, rendering it macroscopic. Moreover, it has shown it to be inherently problematic, such that one cannot remain indifferent towards it. In the society in which Kant was thinking and writing, the community's consensus over the appreciation of a beautiful object could still exist, at least tendentially, as the consensus of humanity in general. For Kant, when I enjoy a beautiful object, I bear witness to and affirm my participation in a community, where this community is the community of humanity itself – albeit thought only as possible, contingent, problematic. Mass culture has by no means standardized aesthetic experience, assimilating the whole of the 'beautiful' to the values of that community which has felt itself to be the privileged bearer of the human – European bourgeois society. Instead, it has explosively brought to light the proliferation of what is 'beautiful', assigning the word not only to different cultures through its anthropological research, but also to 'subsystems' within Western culture itself. In fact, the utopia of an aesthetic rehabilitation of existence through a unification of the beautiful and the everyday has come to an end in parallel with the end of the revolutionary utopia of the sixties, and for the same reasons, namely the explosion of systematicity and the unintelligibility of unilinear history. When history became, or tended towards, universal history – as the excluded, mute and repressed found their voices – it became impossible to think of it as genuinely universal, as unilinear and directed ultimately towards emancipation. Even from an aesthetic perspective, utopia implied a framework of universal history as unilinear. Yet utopia has disappeared, even from aesthetics, with the advent of a certain 'universality' in the channels different models of value and recognition have found to express themselves. As regards aesthetic experience and its relation to everyday life, art has not simply 'retreated' to its place within the modern canon. In addition, a mass aesthetic experience has taken shape in the combined voices raised by communitarian systems of recognition and communities that show, express and recognize themselves in different myths and formal models. In this way, the 'modern' essence of aesthetic experience, which Kant described in the *Critique of Judgement*, is not only made plain as regards its full consequences, but also redefined. The beautiful is the experience of community; but community, when realized as 'universal', is multiplied and undergoes an irreversible pluralization. We live in a society that is intensely aestheticized in precisely the 'Kantian' sense of the word; that is, beauty is realized as the institution of community. Yet by virtue of this very intensification, it seems that the identification of the aesthetic community with the human community *tout court*, which is called for and is tendential at the very least, disappears.

In aesthetics we experience something akin, albeit with different tone and dramatic impact, to what is happening in science, which has always seemed to be where the world is given as a single object (I am still thinking here of the way Habermas speaks of science, where teleological activity presupposes a sole 'objective' world). Our experience, then, is that the world is not one, but many, and what we call the world is perhaps only the 'residual' ambit and regulative horizon (but how problematic) within which worlds are articulated. The aesthetic experience of mass society, the giddy proliferation of 'beautifuls' that make worlds, is likely to be significantly altered by the fact that even the unitary world of which the sciences believed they could speak has revealed itself to be a multiplicity of different worlds. It is no longer possible to speak of aesthetic experience as pure expressivity, as a purely emotive colouring of the world, as one did when the basic world was regarded as a given, open to scientific method of science. This leaves the problem of redefining the nature of aesthetics quite open, and perhaps makes it impossible to 'define it' by delimiting and distinguishing it: here too, it seems we find ourselves before an unforeseen, and perhaps 'distorted' utopia.[8]

Yet the articulation of aesthetic experience as the experience of community, rather than as the appreciation of structures, only occurs in the world of mass culture, diffuse historicism and the end of unitary systems. This is why it is a matter not of a pure and simple realization of utopia, but of a realization that has been distorted and transformed. Aesthetic utopia comes about only through its articulation as *heterotopia*. Our experience of the beautiful in the recognition of models that make world and community is restricted to the moment when these worlds and communities present themselves explicitly as plural. Within this there may lie a normative guideline responding to anxieties that, if the beautiful is only ever the experience of community, we shall no longer have any criterion for distinguishing the violent community of Nazis listening to Wagner from that of rockers geeing themselves up for violence and vandalism, or the community of Beethoven or *Traviata* fans. In arguing that universality as understood by Kant is realized for us only in the form of multiplicity, we can legitimately take plurality lived explicitly as such as a normative criterion. What Kant legitimately, and not just in the false consciousness of ideology, regarded as a call to the universal human community (the expectation that the consensus of each and every human being worthy of the name would coalesce around the values of bourgeois 'beauty'), has in the present conditions of the history of being' become an explicit referral to multiplicity. Self-recognition by groups and communities in their models of beauty involves an intrinsic norm given by the manner in which art and the aesthetic occur, their *Wesen*, in the conditions of our historical destiny; namely, that a community's experience of recognition in a model must explicitly recall – that is, open upon – the multiplicity of models. Admittedly, this is probably to reinstate as exemplary the attitude described by the Nietzsche of the second 'Untimely Meditation' as typical of nineteenth-century man who, the product of an exaggeratedly historical culture, wandered like a tourist through the garden of history, continually seeking different disguises as though he were in a theatrical costumier's.[9] Aesthetic experience becomes inauthentic when, in the context of this giddy plurality of models, a group's self-recognition in its own models is experienced and presented in the form of an identification of the community with humanity itself. That is, when the beautiful is experienced, presented, and recognized by the community in question as an absolute value. The possible 'truth' of late-modern aesthetic experience is probably that of 'collectionism', the fickleness of fashion and the museum. In the end it is the market itself, where objects circulate that have demythologized the reference to use value and have become pure exchange value – not necessarily monetary exchange alone, but also symbolic exchange, as status

From Utopia to Heterotopia

symbols and tokens of group recognition. It would not be too rash, perhaps, to suggest that many of the theoretical discourses of philosophical aesthetics and art criticism today are explicable as attempts to prolong, in spite of everything, the validity of 'structural' criteria with respect to works of art. But not all theories are so exorcistical and regressively evasive. Beginning with Dilthey, whose theses are also found in Ricoeur, and still earlier in Heidegger, the capacity of the work of art to 'make world' is always thought of in the plural – thus not in the utopian sense, but in the heterotopian sense. Indeed, in 'The origin of the work of art' (1936) Heidegger no longer speaks of *the* world, as in *Being and Time*, but of *a* world (and so implicitly of many worlds). And Dilthey himself saw aesthetic (and historiographic) experience as deeply significant by virtue of its capacity to make us live, in the realm of the imagination, other possibilities of existence, thereby extending the borders of the specific possibility we realize in everydayness.[10] For Heidegger, one has only to leave the still fundamentally scientific horizon within which Dilthey operates in order to see the meaning of aesthetic experience in the opening of *a world* or *worlds*, where these are not 'just' imaginary, but constitute being itself, that is, are events of being.

This reading, or rather outline, of the transformation in aesthetic experience over the last twenty years may be brought to a close, albeit provisionally, by setting out two implications of what has already been said.

The most eye-catching feature of the passage from utopia to heterotopia is the liberation of ornament and the lightening of being which is its ontological significance. The liberation of ornament, or better still the discovery of the ornamental character of the aesthetic, the ornamental essence of the beautiful, is the very meaning of the heterotopia of aesthetic experience. The beautiful is not a site wherein truth is manifest and finds sensible, provisional, anticipatory and educative expression, as the tradition of metaphysical aesthetics has often wished were the case. Beauty is ornament, in the sense that its essential significance, the interest to which it responds, is the extention of life's world through a process of referrals to other possible life worlds. These, however, are not merely imaginary, marginal or complementary to the real world, but comprise and constitute the so-called real world in their reciprocal play and as their residue. The ornamental essence of the culture of mass society, the ephemeral quality of its products, the eclecticism by which it is dominated, the impossibility of identifying anything essential – which often leads to talk of *Kitsch* in connection with this culture – fully corresponds to the *Wesen* of the aesthetic of late modernity. That is, it is not on the basis of a return to 'structural' evaluations, focused on the beautiful object, that one can be selective with regard to this culture. *Kitsch*, if it exists at all, is not what falls short of rigorous formal criteria and whose inauthentic presentation lacks a strong style. Rather, *Kitsch* is simply that which, in the age of plural ornamentation, still wishes to stand like a monument more lasting than bronze and still lays claim to the stability, definitive character and perfection of 'classic' art. It would not be an exaggeration to say that neither aesthetic theory nor critique seem equipped to achieve a selective orientation in the world of late-modern aesthetics *juxta propria principia*, that is, without the persistent and irremediably ideological reference to the structure of the object. Whether and to what extent this insufficiency on the part of aesthetics and critique actually exists is debatable. But if it does, which is my view, it probably

From Utopia to Heterotopia

also depends on a failure to acknowledge the second 'implication' of the transition in aesthetic experience from utopia to heterotopia, namely the ontological consequences. This is the source of the extraordinary importance of Heidegger's 'ontology' for our thought. It alone seems capable of opening us authentically to the experience of late modernity without a persistent implicit reference to metaphysical canons and principles. In the case of aesthetics this may be seen precisely in the way it is wholly incapable of considering the aesthetic experience of mass culture not as a mere perversion of authentic values and essences but as a fateful opportunity. Benjamin's efforts in the essay on 'The work of art in the age of mechanical reproduction' led in this direction, but were probably too tightly bound to a dialectical conception of reality for them to succeed. Heidegger, on the contrary, in his critique of the metaphysical identification of being with the object and the structural stability of the 'given', radically delegitimizes nostalgia for both classic form and evaluations based on structure. Only if being is not to be thought of as the ground and stability of eternal structures, but presents itself rather as event, with all the implications this carries with it – principally a fundamental weakening, whereby being *is not*, but *happens* – only on these conditions may aesthetic experience as heterotopia, as the proliferation of ornament, as unfounding of the world (in the sense of both its being placed against a background and its comprehensive de-authorization),[11] acquire meaning and become the theme of a radical theoretical reflection. Without this reference to ontology, any attempt to read the transformations in aesthetic experience of the last two decades (or, indeed, of previous ages) as a calling and a 'destiny' would appear to be a mere historical whimsy, a concession to fashion, the weakness of one who must at all costs keep pace with the times. Yet, as we know, that times have a pace and clear direction depends on their being read, interpreted. The wager on heterotopia, so to speak, will escape being merely frivolous, if it can link the transformed aesthetic experience of mass society with Heidegger's call to an experience of being that is (at last) non-metaphysical. Only if, following Heidegger, we can somehow gauge that being is precisely what is not, is precisely what dissolves, affirms itself in its difference insofar as it is not present, only then, perhaps, can we find a way amidst the explosion of the ornamental and heterotopian character of today's aesthetic.

NOTES

1 Cf. esp. J. Dewey, *Art as Experience* (Minton, Balch & Co., New York, 1934). On Dewey's aesthetics, cf. R. Barilli's superb study *Per una estetica mondana* (Il Mulino, Bologna, 1964).
2 T. Adorno, *Aesthetic Theory* (1970), tr. C. Lenhardt, ed. G. Adorno and R. Tiedemann (Routledge & Kegan Paul, London, 1984).
3 As well as H. Marcuse's classic *Eros and Civilization: A Philosophical Inquiry into Freud* (Beacon Press, Boston, 1955), it is worth referring to the essays collected in *Kultur und Gesellschaft* (Suhrkamp, Frankfurt a. M. 1965), and *The Aesthetic Dimension: Toward a Critique of Marxist Aesthetics* (1977), tr. and revised by H. Marcuse and E. Sherover (Beacon Press, Boston, 1978).
4 H. Lefebvre, *Critique of Everyday Life* (1947), tr. J. Moore (Verso Editions, London, 1991).
5 E. Bloch, *Geist der Utopie* (1918/1923), *Gesamtausgabe*, vol. 16 (Suhrkamp, Frankfurt a. M., 1971).
6 J. Habermas, *Theory of Communicative Action*, vol. 2 (1985), tr. T. McCarthy, (Beacon Press, Boston, 1985).

7 Apart from Gadamer's *Truth and Method*, which we have already cited, cf. *The Relevance of the Beautiful*, tr. N. Walker, ed. R. Bernasconi (Cambridge University Press, 1986).
8 This 'distortion' is considered on the basis of a central term in Heidegger's philosophy, *Verwindung*. With regard to metaphysics, that is, the oblivion of being, thought can only carry out a 'twisting free' that also follows and accepts the tradition in some way. In connection with all of this, cf. the last chapter of my *End of Modernity* (1985), tr. J. Snyder (Polity Press, Cambridge, 1988).
9 F. Nietzsche, 'On the uses and disadvantages of history for life', the second of the *Untimely Meditations* (1874), tr. R. J. Hollingdale (Cambridge University Press, 1983).
10 Cf. the essays collected in W. Dilthey, *Der Aufbau der geschichtlichen Welt in den Geisteswissenschaften* (Teubner, Leipzig, 1927), and *Studien zur Grundlegung der Geisteswissenschaften* (Reichsdruckerei, Berlin, 1905).
11 [Cf. ch. 4 n. 9 – Trans.]

6

Utopia, Counter-utopia, Irony

It has been rightly observed that an essential feature of the twentieth-century utopia has been the rise and dissemination of that literary genre variously described as anti-utopia, dis-utopia, counter-utopia.[1] Indeed, this is perhaps not just *one* of the features of the twentieth-century utopia, but rather *the* salient feature, at least to judge from the consistency with which literature and other utopian art-forms, the cinema above all, have produced 'perfectly negative' images of the world that nonetheless retain the 'optimizing' character of utopia. By this I mean that they imagine a reality in which what are at present only possibilities are realized in all their most extreme implications. But instead of a world of perfect happiness, all this gives rise to quite the contrary, to a total and irremediable unhappiness. The negativity of the twentieth-century counter-utopia is more radical and total compared to the models of counter-utopia one finds in works such as *Gulliver's Travels*. Its form is not that of an *exemplum*, warning against dangers and distortions inherent in the possible consequences of actual facts and circumstances. Works such as Fritz Lang's *Metropolis* (1926), George Orwell's

Utopia, Counter-utopia, Irony

Nineteen Eighty Four (1948 – this too has been made into a film recently) and Huxley's *Brave New World* (1932), which have become emblematic of the twentieth-century counter-utopia, have a radicality that distinguishes them from all the counter-utopias of the past. Is this radicality explicable on the basis of the twentieth century's negative experiences of politics, the military application of technology and the failure and perversion of, amongst others, the communist revolution? We know that all these factors were essential to the birth of counter-utopias. The climate of catastrophe surrounding the counter-utopia of expressionist cinema is clearly deeply marked by what were then the still recent experiences of the First World War. The demands of wartime military production had led, perhaps for the first time, to the highly rigid and alienated organization of industrial work, and consequently of social discipline as well. Hence, Orwell's *Nineteen Eighty Four* reflects not only the experiences of European Fascism in the thirties, but also, and far more profoundly, the impact of Stalinist totalitarianism on the liberal consciousness of the time.

In my view, however, it would be misleading to trace the rise of counter-utopia in the literature and collective imaginary of our century back to these disappointments, to the type of negative experiences we have mentioned. At bottom, these are never more than 'partial' explanations. Even the current and tragically well-founded fear of an impending nuclear destruction or the ecological devastation of the planet is not enough to justify the radicality with which the utopian imagination produces its models of perfect negativity. The counter-utopia characteristic of our century makes one think rather of more global factors than those going back to the specific negative, and particularly painful, experiences humanity has undergone recently. That which has occurred, manifesting itself in counter-utopia, may be defined as the emergence of the *counter-finality of reason* – of what, in their 1947 book, Horkheimer and Adorno called the *Dialectic of Enlightenment*. It is not simply that certain negative experiences (the two world wars and the innumerable local wars where ever more sophisticated weapons of death are deployed, the intensive exploitation of the planet's resources to the brink of exhaustion, the new and unlimited possibilities of control provided by electronics) have led us to realize that 'progress', above all in technological terms, *can* lead to consequences that are catastrophic for life. Such a possibility is fully within the compass of tradition: technical advances have always brought with them the possibility of their wrongful application, or have given rise to risks that were previously unknown. By contrast, our own situation seems to be characterized by something more general. Although it stands before our very eyes, to grasp it requires a particularly concerted reflection: it is the discovery that the rationalization of the world turns against reason and its ends of perfection and emancipation, and does so not by error, accident, or a chance distortion, but precisely to the extent that it is more and more perfectly accomplished.

If it holds, such a hypothesis retrospectively throws a different light on the past history of utopia. For example, it leads us to see the strict connection between it and the history of modern rationalism. To be sure, beginning with Plato, there are utopian texts that do not strictly form part of the history of modern rationalism (though according to a broader view going back to Nietzsche or Heidegger, this history may quite legitimately feature Plato as well, indeed, above all). But if we think of the proper and more historically precise meaning of the term utopia, of the island described by Thomas More in the work which gave the term the sense it has for us today, we immediately find ourselves within the history of modern rationalist thought. The reality outlined by Thomas More, or by Campanella in his *Città del Sole*, is not 'optimized' on the basis of images inspired by an immediate and naive desire for well-being and happiness. Rather, they *deduce* the features of their ideal world from a rational and systematic recognition of the essence of humanity, its possibilities and its calling. Whereas the rationality one sees in More, and above all in Campanella, is based on the recognition of essences as normative ideals that give rise to what may be called a metaphysical utopia, in Francis Bacon's *New Atlantis* (published posthumously in 1627) it becomes a technological utopia availing itself of all the possibilities put at humanity's disposal by the known machines of the time. But there is a deep-seated relationship between these two kinds of utopia, and it lies in their nature as reality optimized by rational design. Nobody uses the term utopia to depict the country of Bengodi, a random image of a happy world, like a retrospective mythical golden age at the dawn of history. Properly speaking, the term utopia concerns the realization of an optimal reality by way of rational design, whether it be oriented metaphysically (as in Campanella) or technologically (as in Bacon).

In this way, utopia reveals its own relationship with modern rationalism, or with what Heidegger would call the will to system. As we know, in Heidegger's view metaphysics is that thinking which treats being as a system of objects rigorously connected to one another by the principle of causality. In ancient metaphysics – above all in Aristotle – this concatenation of all beings according to the nexus of foundation is grasped only at the level of an ideal in the mind whereas in modernity it is actually made real through the operation of technology, which is thereby the realization of metaphysics. Now, when seen as specifically modern in origin, utopia is effectively an aspect of the will to system proper to metaphysics. One could call it a metaphysical rationalism, or a Hegelianism, switched around into the future. Ernst Bloch, the major 'utopian' thinker of our time, understands utopia this way. In his famous book on Hegel,[2] Bloch does not reproach Hegel for his will to system and the manner in which he regards the totality as a possible truth, but for the anamnestic character of his thinking, for the fact that he regards the totality, the system, as in principle already complete. For Bloch, too, the true remains the whole, the all, outside of which there is nothing but error and alienation. But the whole does not stand behind us as something already realized; rather, it is the utopian *telos* grasped by anticipatory consciousness. One may go so far as to think, as in fact Adorno has done with greater radicality, that the utopian *telos* understood in this way cannot even be delineated. This would suggest a kind of prohibition – analogous to that in the Old Testament against making images, or even pronouncing the name, of God – outlawing every possibility of forming a positive idea of what the utopian *telos* contains. It is difficult to say whether such an iconoclastic conception of the utopian *telos* as Adorno's is in agreement with Bloch's view. Nonetheless, in its most radically negative form, namely Adorno's, utopia still maintains a link with the totality that one could never imagine realized. Even when it is nothing more than a critical principle warning against the pretensions of all historical realizations, the utopian *telos* displays close links with the totality and thereby the metaphysical will to system.

Utopia, Counter-utopia, Irony

If the utopian imagination is properly speaking not purely and simply a flight of fantasy to a happier world, but rather a constitutive feature of the modern metaphysical mind, as one can quite reasonably argue, then what meaning are we to attach to the twentieth-century utopia and the fact that it takes the form above all of a counter-utopia? With the discovery of the counter-finality of reason, which is lived in the collective imaginary via the affirmation of counter-utopias, it is not only isolated errors or risks of corruption that are experienced and exhibited; it is the very mechanism of rationalization that is 'suspended', thrown into crisis and under accusation worldwide. It is apparently no longer by chance that counter-utopia comes to the fore in an age when, at the level of common consciousness, there is a marked dissolution of the ideology of progress (inspired by the same experiences of 'counter-finality' that inspire counter-utopia). But this is not all: progress no longer makes any sense as a dogma of the philosophy of history because it is precisely history as *unilinear* that is no longer intelligible, except at the price of grave ideological violence. One may recall Benjamin's 'Theses on the Philosophy of History', and also Bloch's 'Differenzierungen im Begriff Fortschritt'.[3] To be sure, philosophy, initially in Nietzsche, then in Heidegger, but also in a less 'aural'[4] thinker such as Adorno (with his insistence that humanity and its thought can never be the same 'after Auschwitz'), feels itself to be witnessing an epochal turning-point in humanity. Moreover, philosophers as different as Adorno and Heidegger agree that the discovery of the counter-finality of reason is the stamp of this turning-point. It is no longer simply a matter of the possible rebellion against humanity of a single technological mechanism, or even of an entire system of machines – like the robots of expressionist fantasy. The counter-finality of reason consists in the fact that, even when realizing itself 'correctly' and according to plan, reason turns against the very ends of emancipation and 'humanization' by which it is motivated. Clearly, one cannot respond to this discovery by taking another step down the path of a fuller and more authentic rationalization, for it is precisely this mechanism that has shown itself to be corrupt. In *The Dialectic of Enlightenment*, Horkheimer and Adorno implied that it may be possible to correct, as it were, the corruption of reason by way of a 'critique of instrumental reason'. Reason, that is, had gone astray, giving rise to a totally administered world, to the manipulation of consciousness etc., because it had chosen scientific, objectifying, metrical reason as its model. Adorno, harking back to Weberian theses, viewed the predominance of objective, calculative, instrumental reason as linked to the imposition on society of the capitalist order. It could be hoped, then, that an emancipation of society from capitalism could lead to a less unilaterally calculative and instrumental practice of reason as well, opening the way forward to a different form of rationalization that could retrieve some sense of liberation. Yet in the years that followed the 1947 work, Adorno's thought took a different direction, towards the critical-negative utopianism we mentioned earlier. The hope for an emancipation of reason from its modern historical 'figure', with its mix of social discipline, repression, calculative objectivization and the technological application of science, has seemed less and less realistic. Instead, it has increasingly seemed that the utopian *telos* can be affirmed only in negative terms.

Contemporary philosophy is ever more clearly aware of the manifest counter-finality of reason. But where

Utopia, Counter-utopia, Irony

does this awareness lead? And for their part, do the experiences of the utopian imagination give any indication of the path thought is to take, once it has recognized that the mechanism of linear and progressive rationalization has jammed, entangled in self-contradiction?

Concerning this last point, it is interesting to reflect on the cinemagraphic utopia of the last few years. Ridley Scott's celebrated film *Blade Runner*, released in 1983, is generally acknowledged to be the model for a whole string of films (beginning before this film, in fact, with works such as *1997 Escape from New York* or various survival epics, inaugurated by the final unforgettable scene of *The Planet of the Apes*), in which the set-design and pace of the action contribute to a projection of the future in the light of ruins. The lasting impression of *Blade Runner* is not of the events themselves (the hunt for the 'replicants', robots in human form that rebel against the 'termination date' pre-set by their constructors), but rather of a city (Los Angeles?) with all the architectural features of an enormous archaeological park of twentieth-century buildings. It is not without good reason that there has been talk of a postmodern scenographic imagination. The backdrop of ruins, as we see more clearly in other films, is justified by the fact that the events being recounted, which are often banal and of a very 'traditionally' violent nature, are set in a time when the atomic apocalypse has already occurred. The utopia of contemporary cinematography may be said to have a truly post-apocalyptic thread. The fact that it is a matter of utopia seems not to be in doubt. This is not only for the somewhat banal reason that the events are set in the future, in a future that is thought to be determined by taking to their extremes those elements of technical

Utopia, Counter-utopia, Irony

and scientific progress that characterize our lives at present. Above all, it is a matter of utopia because, paradoxically, the post-apocalyptic condition these works describe is in some sense a happy one; that is, at least the atomic catastrophe that weighs upon us as a constant threat is imagined to have happened already, and for the survivors this somehow amounts to a form of liberation. A sense of liberation – albeit, as ever, paradoxical – also cloaks the retreat from technology and its products within the post-apocalyptic genre. The reasons behind the break are not necessarily ethico-rational, and it is fairly clear that the justification is felt to lie in the fact that the catastrophe the survivors have just put behind them was, one imagines, produced with the aid of the very technological apparatus that is constitutive of the world of rationalization. In the general ruin of the post-apocalyptic world, the retreat from all technological apparatus – still there, though not functioning too brilliantly – is ultimately ironic in tone, as in certain scenes from Woody Allen's *Sleeper* (which probably does not actually belong to the post-apocalyptic genre, however). Owing to all these features – the apocalypse having already occurred, the world of 'progress' in ruins, the ironic-nostalgic retreat from that world, which often also means a break with its rhythms and a general slowing in the pace of action – the counter-utopia we are proposing to call post-apocalyptic bears more than a superficial resemblance to non-'progressionist' elements of earlier utopias that were registered, not so much in literature and theory, as in the practice of protest groups in the late sixties. The 'flower children' of the California campuses sought to achieve a way of life that was closer to nature, ecologically balanced, non-repressive and yet also, inseparably, non-violent. Above all, they disengaged

Utopia, Counter-utopia, Irony

from the myths of production by implicitly choosing 'zero growth'. These are all attitudes that, in substance, are often to be found in the post-apocalyptic genre, which itself represents a sort of forced return to a 'natural' condition. However, this is to be understood neither as a new terrestrial paradise, nor as a pure and simple collapse into barbarism. The return to nature, here, bears traces, cultivated with an ironic nostalgia, of the 'progress' that has been achieved. It might be said that the atomic catastrophe, which in this type of utopia has halted what was once thought to be the unstoppable course of progress, leads ultimately to the mass of artefacts of the world of advanced technology being treated inventorially, with a contemplative attitude akin to that in Schopenhauer's description of the aesthetic contemplation of ideas. It's worth trying to describe the mood that arises when confronted with films like these, for it can probably tell us more than most theories about the 'post-historical'[5] character of what seems to be the present human condition. The significance of post-apocalyptic counter-utopias lies ultimately in their shaping an existence that is no longer historical. Not in the sense of the happy return to nature of certain utopian fantasies of the past, but rather in the sense, conforming more strictly to the modern conception of utopia, of representing an accomplishment, a passage to the extremes, based on a full realization of what is, for now, our (only) possibility. The ironic-nostalgic inventory of the talismans of progress is perhaps the only 'utopia' still possible. It is perhaps the only future condition of humanity that can be imagined and, up to a point, described in later modernity, after the hopes humanity placed in the rationalization and progressive enlightenment of the world have worn thin before its very eyes. The difficulties involved in continuing to describe this condition as a utopia – for example, in deciding whether it concerns that admixture of foresight and optative, wishful anticipation that has characterized utopia in the past – are due entirely to the fact that our present situation is one where, for the first time since the completion of the history of metaphysics and its will to system, there emerges a 'utopia' outside any perspective of linear, and thus potentially progressive, temporality. Moreover, with the end of metaphysics and the faith in progress, utopia's only possible content is that of inventory, nostalgia, *revival*. Yet even from the point of view of its emotive worth, this condition no longer has the appearance of a 'completion' or achievement (corresponding to a course of events and the satisfaction of an active tension) of something desirable or final, in the teleological sense. Post-historical humanity no longer regards the course of history with the tension of hope or fear that characterized humanity dominated by the linear experience of time. From this point of view, our interpretation of the meaning of the post-apocalyptic utopia may have something else to learn from Adorno's *Dialectic of Enlightenment*. The motives for Adorno's revival and transformation of dialectic, to the point where it becomes 'negative dialectic', are not primarily logical or systematic. Dialectic in its Hegelian form is not abandoned because it is contradictory or somehow conceptually unsatisfactory; Adorno's sole reason for thinking that 'the whole is false', and not that 'truth is the whole', in contrast to Hegel, is that in the century and a half separating us from Hegel, the whole has become real: the rational totalization of the world has been realized, in principle at least. Once more, Adorno is closer to Heidegger, here, than he would care to think. The world's total organization and its domination by an instrumental rationality capable of exercising an almost all-embracing discipline on society is precisely what Heidegger described as the completion of metaphysics. Adorno, as we have seen, still hoped that the levelling out of reason to its instrumental and dominant form could be corrected and that, via a comprehensive transformation of society, rationalization could know a new emancipatory destiny. But this conviction gave way more and more explicitly to the growing negativity of the utopia and, effectively, to the rejection of every philosophy of history. However, in the idea that the whole is false precisely to the extent that it is realized there lies a new philosophy of history in embryonic form. This would be characterized by the replacement of the linear (ascending, descending, progressive or regressive) and the cyclic models, pertaining respectively to the Hebraic–Christian vision of history and the classical model of time, with one that could only be defined as ironic and distortive, and which may be traced back in the context of contemporary philosophy to certain 'nihilistic' effects of hermeneutics.[6] Historical occurrence, in other words, would be neither progress nor regress nor even the return of the same, but an 'interpretation' in which the past and the principles we inherit always become in some degree false. Such a model, at least in our hypothesis, is not applicable solely to the rationalization of society and the exposure of counter-finality that goes with it. Its roots seem to sink deeper, into the whole of modern history, which, not by chance, is often presented in the form of 'secularization'. This concept, whose fecundity for the possible reconstruction of the philosophy of history has yet to be explored,[7] has less to do with the overturning of a sacred order that is no longer accepted, or with leaving such an order behind as an error that has now been recognized and eliminated, and more to do with a relation of repetition–maintenance–distortion – a relation that is precisely typical of the links between modern profane society and its Hebraic–Christian roots. Secularization is exemplified here by the relation Max Weber established between Hebraic–Christian monotheism in general, and the Protestant ethic in particular, and the development of Western capitalism or, simply, modernity itself.[8] In modern capitalism the Christian ethic is not simply left behind as something false and useless. Rather, it is 'realized', albeit in a form the early followers of Jesus would have difficulty recognizing. It is this ethic that 'articulates' the capitalist world, which cannot 'be otherwise' than it is. Indeed, its most real historical presence, thus also its truest, is precisely this, as opposed to its preservation (but with what degree of authenticity?) as a collection of precepts bearing less and less relation to the 'truth', as they are set in forms that belong to the past and are less and less applicable to life as it is.

As a post-apocalyptic utopia, and we have only touched upon this here, the utopian imagination of recent years seems to go beyond the discovery of the counter-finality of reason and rediscover the possibility, albeit paradoxical, of a projection onto the 'future': a future *sui generis*, which must be defined within the bounds of a conception of history that is no longer either linear or circular, but ironic-hermeneutico-distortive, and which philosophy and culture, with the help of the utopian imagination, is only now beginning to approach and explore.

Utopia, Counter-utopia, Irony

NOTES

1. V. Verra, 'Utopia', in *Enciclopedia del Novecento*, vol. 7 (Institute della Enciclopedia Italiana, Rome, 1984), p. 1004.
2. E. Bloch, *Subjekt–Objekt: Erläuterungen zu Hegel, Gesamtausgabe*, vol. 8, (Suhrkamp, Frankfurt a. M., 1962).
3. W. Benjamin, 'Theses on the Philosophy of History', in *Illuminations*, tr. H. Zorn, ed. H. Arendt (Jonathan Cape, London, 1982). Bloch's essay ['Differentiations in the concept of progress' – Trans.] is a written address dating back to 1955, in Gesamtausgabe, vol. 13. Concerning these matters, see my 'Il tempo nella filosofia del Novecento', in N. Tranfaglia (ed.), *Il mondo contemporaneo* (La Nuova Italia, Florence, 1983).
4. [The term refers Benjamin's understanding of 'aura': cf. above, p. 46 – Trans.]
5. A. Gehlen, *Die Säkulisierung des Fortschritt*, in *Gesamtausgabe*, ed. K. S. Rehberg, vol. 7: *Einblike* (Frankfurt a. M., Klostermann, 1978).
6. For a fuller discussion of this topic, as well as its connection with the notion of *Verwindung* (repetition–maintainance–distortion) elaborated in Heidegger, may I refer the reader again to my *End of Modernity* (1985), tr. J. Snyder (Polity Press, Cambridge, 1988).
7. For an introduction to the history of this concept, cf. H. Lubbe, *Säkulisierung: Geschichte eines ideenpolitischen Begriffs* (Alber, Freiburg, 1965).
8. M. Weber, *The Protestant Ethic and the Spirit of Capitalism* (1930), tr. T. Parsons (Allen & Unwin, London, 1985).

7

Disenchantment and Dissolution

Is what is lacking in politics, and the politics of the left in particular, a well-founded theory to give force and logical coherence to programmes of progressive action? In an essay entitled 'Disenchantment betrayed', Paolo Flores d'Arcais seems to assume something of the kind, at least implicitly.[1] Yet the disenchantment, whether betrayed or not, that characterizes modernity has also involved a transformation in the relation between theory and practice, owing to the very concepts of 'theoretical project' and foundation breaking down. Flores is clearly aware of this when he admits that one cannot reinstate the discourse of natural law, and that it is rather a matter of choosing (or finding reasons for choosing) to be faithful to the project of modernity, irrespective of any possibility of founding this choice on apodictic argument. In place of a foundation, Flores proposes a 'call' to fidelity. However, this way of reasoning may itself have presuppositions and corollaries that imply a different understanding of the theory–praxis relation, and in particular of the relation between philosophy and politics. The project of modernity, characterized by disenchantment, itself

Disenchantment and Dissolution

comprises the impossibility of founding the fidelity we 'owe' it on a cogent demonstration. Moreover, and precisely because we are no longer within the horizon of logic and cogency, the 'political' significance of philosophy is less direct. Indeed, what occasionally grates in Flores's discourse on disenchantment is actually a residual aspiration to a foundational role for theory, at least with respect to practice. The majority of the points Flores makes in his essay, whether they are programmatic suggestions or empirical critique, may of course be shared without any qualms. What seems less faithful to the meaning of disenchantment is the effort to derive it from a generally theoretical orientation. Not that the discourse lacks logical coherence. It is rather the reader (and not just a specific reader, myself) who lacks the inclination to treat political problems as resolvable in the light of a correct theory, indeed in the light of any theory essentially. The disenchantment of the world to which we are supposed to be faithful also comprises a certain scepticism, or at least an experience of the obliqueness of the relation between theory and practice. The betrayal of disenchantment and the failure of the project of modernity are not born principally from the 'defects' of theory: nor can the revival of this project and the most radical fidelity to disenchantment be accomplished as 'consequences' or 'applications' of a correct theory.

However, we could adopt another view of theory. From the perspective of disenchantment, it could be seen as a 'rhetorical accessory', a kind of 'supplement of the soul', or an indispensable discursive apparatus aimed at preparing and sustaining both a politics and, above all, a living morality capable of keeping strict faith with disenchantment. Such a conception of theory does not absolve us from the obligation of arguing – rhetorically,

Disenchantment and Dissolution

if not 'scientifically' – for certain values being preferable to others. It simply frees us from one of the characteristic legacies of the left, namely the pretence of legitimizing even the most contingent and 'technical' political decisions (think of certain decisions regarding the Soviet five-year plans in the Stalinist era), by appealing to precise theoretical coordinates. Provisionally, then, for we shall come back to this later, we can say that the transformation of the theory–praxis relation is one of the aspects of disenchantment that will have to be taken into account. This seems to be essential to the operation of democracy, for without a radical awareness of this transformation, democracy will always seem to be merely a 'lesser evil', entrusting to the majority decisions that, 'strictly', that is, according to a foundational conception of rationality, should follow from logically cogent argumentation – with all the consequences such thinking may have, not least for the power that scientists and technicians are understood to wield in society. Disenchantment is also, and inseparably, a less forceful presence in society and politics than theory and its rules of logical construction. A theoretical treatment of disenchantment must bear this is mind, above all with regard to its own manner of presentation and formulation.

Is disenchantment simply what Karl Löwith describes when he says that modern man is disenchanted insofar as he knows the world does not have an 'objective meaning' and that it falls to man 'primarily to create objective meaning, and the interconnection of meaning, the relation to reality, insofar as *his* relation is to *create* meaning theoretically and practically'?[2] In this light, the project of modernity characterized by disenchantment appears to be defined in terms of praxis or, one could say with Heidegger, 'humanism'. Not only is the world not populated by gods (and can therefore be conceived as the huge machine in which techno-science and capitalist rationalization install themselves), but nor can it be apprehended as an objective given order. In any case, whatever the differences between the objectively cogent 'necessity' of the 'natural' *Müssen* and the autonomy of the moral sphere may be, it is certain that the human world of ethics and politics at least cannot be drawn back to 'given' laws, but only to what humanity, as free, makes of itself. The other quotation from Löwith that Flores opportunely recalls ('Science itself cannot decide whether there should be this or that special science, or whether there should be science as such: *only the individual can decide* for or against this'[3]) hands the responsibility for creating and deciding back to the *individual*. According to Flores, however, the passage from disenchantment to equality is neither linear nor logically necessary.

> Once God, in whatever form, is exiled, we are faced with the following dilemma. As there is only the individual, *One* is master of the law, to the negation of all others (who feature only as enemies or subjects). Alternatively, as the individual is *merely* the individual, each is master of the law in the sense that everyone shares in it equally. Whether the individual is to be understood in the first or the second sense remains *undecidable* in the light of rationality.[4]

Although, strictly, the alternative may be implausible, it seems clear to Flores that the first sense of the individual, the 'egocratic' sense, is 'regressive' because the modern world, through the history of its revolutions, has explicitly chosen the egalitarian reading. This historically progressive alternative is to be preferred, we are told, in the name of a duty to be 'faithful' to the

Disenchantment and Dissolution

modern tradition, for which no further argument is offered.

That there may not be an ultimate foundation is no scandal. In order to gain a deeper understanding of disenchantment and its 'implications', one could, perhaps, analyse further what is involved in the recommendation of fidelity to the choice modernity has made. If it is a matter of recommending fidelity and not of demonstrating an inevitable logical consequence, it is immediately clear that only the second, egalitarian, alternative can be the object of a recommendation. Suppose modernity had made the 'egocratic' choice instead: would there be any sense in declaring that it must be followed not on account of logical reasons, but on faith? To speak of faith rather than logical necessity is a way of practising disenchantment. But can one preach authoritarianism in the name of disenchantment? It seems a vision of rationality which acknowledges the impossibility of an 'ultimate foundation' and presents itself as a call to a 'vocation' or historical 'sending' cannot but tend towards the egalitarian alternative. In a disenchanted logic, one cannot be 'faithful' to the egocratic alternative of a violent and subjugatory reading of the responsibility of man to create meaning. This logic is not restricted to acknowledging that there is no such thing as an objective order of reality, whereupon it falls to man to create meaning. It immediately outlaws any pretensions to authoritarianism and is directed towards consensus amongst equals in both its form and its content, dispelling the 'possible' reading inclined towards oppression.

If this is so, it is significant in that it adds to disenchantment what proves to be an essential connotation – and not from outside, by chance or accident: namely, to the extent that it takes responsibility for the

Disenchantment and Dissolution

creation of meaning, disenchantment assumes the form of a decision for non-violence. There is no foundation for subordinating oneself to a *given* and transcendent objective order, nor for subordinating oneself to someone who could demand obedience in the name of that order alone. In the world without foundations, everyone is equal and the imposition of any system of meaning on others is violence and oppression, for it can never legitimate itself by referring to an objective order. The only possible foundation for the predominance of an order of meaning is force.

At this point, however, disenchantment seems to strike a limit that is hard to ignore, although Flores seems to do just that. First, it is admitted that the alternative between 'egocracy' and egalitarianism is undecidable, and then it is agreed that one should prefer equality solely out of faith to choices modernity has *already made*. Disenchantment, thought radically, *has reasons* for excluding the alternative of oppression and egocracy. Yet in so doing, it also highlights the fact that the plain espousal of equality, if it is genuinely disenchanted, has no rational arguments with which to oppose the reduction of reality, or at least the human world of ethics and politics, to a pure play of forces. The various ways in which, above all, the 'weak' have tried to exorcize their awareness of this have been swept aside by disenchantment: metaphysical theories of man, world, God, foundation, essence etc. are all ways of masking the senselessness of reality. Once this has become clear, what remains? Precisely equality as perfect formal reciprocity. But nothing states that such a reciprocity, where views are upheld by reason, need not also allow that they may be upheld by force.

The only way of avoiding these (not so) paradoxical consequences of disenchantment – a theme introduced to the West primarily by Nietzsche under the name of nihilism – is to rethink its causes and meaning still more radically (than Flores d'Arcais does in his essay). If the Enlightenment, which is another name for disenchantment as the programme of modernity, is inspired by epistemological motives alone, it is unlikely to avoid the perverse dialectic described in definitive terms by Horkheimer and Adorno. But the Enlightenment, or disenchantment, is not anti-authoritarian, egalitarian and libertarian because it has 'discovered' the true metaphysical basis of things. Rather, it sets about exposing metaphysics precisely because it is anti-authoritarian and libertarian. This shift in emphasis in the conception of disenchantment has important consequences, which amount, perhaps, to saying that even when the superficial and provisional character of disenchantment's concern with knowledge has been exposed, it is found to be moved principally by an *ethical* requirement to emerge from violence and oppression. But this requirement cannot be satisfied simply by establishing equality and reciprocity, founded solely on a sort of formalism of reason.[5]

To the extent that communicative reciprocity is indeed disenchanted, there is no apparent 'reason' why it should not end up as the extreme nihilism described by Nietzsche, for example in the long Lenzer Heide fragment of June 1887.[6] In this note, which is part of the unfinished texts of Nietzsche's final period originally destined for the unwritten *Will to Power*, Nietzsche describes nihilism precisely in terms of disenchantment: the rationalization of social existence made possible by morals, metaphysics and religion – that is, belief in God, the objective order of the world, etc. – has led European man to see what a sham morals, metaphysics and religion are themselves. God is too extreme an hypothesis and is no longer necessary with the security, albeit relative, we enjoy today by virtue of the very changes in social life made possible by the 'hypothesis' of God. The same goes for metaphysics and for morality founded on supposedly natural laws. Disenchantment is the recognition that there *are* no objective structures, values or laws and that everything is posited, created by man (at least in the realm of meaning). Accordingly, one can no longer avoid (as metaphysics in its various forms has always done, claiming to have grasped objective structures) the recognition that there is nothing but the play of forces. Yet here, where the weak can do nothing but perish, the best is reserved not for the most violent but rather for 'the most moderate, those that have no need for faith in extreme principles . . . those who know how to diminish the value of humanity in their thinking, yet without becoming little and weak'. If one reads Nietzsche's late notes carefully, it would appear possible to make sense of this leap towards an ideal of moderation, which is certainly at odds with the current image of his thought. It is a matter of a kind of return to Schopenhauer, who was in fact so important in the formation of Nietzsche's early thought.[7] In Nietzsche, the exposure of the will to power concealed within every claim to have grasped an objective order, and thus the exposure of the non-existence of such an order – what Löwith calls the recognition that meaning is not given but must be created by man – does not give rise to the exaltation of force pure and simple (as his Nazi and Fascist interpreters would have it), but rather to a shift in attention towards the 'more moderate' man. At first blush, this shift seems justified by the fact that, as witnessed by the whole of the Western tradition, the play of forces has always operated solely by masking itself behind metaphysical legitimations. It seems that

Disenchantment and Dissolution

once violence is uncovered, it no longer achieves its aims; just as lying becomes useless and impossible in a situation where everyone is lying. However, we can ask ourselves why the exposure and exacerbation of violence – that is, disenchantment – should lead to such a dialectical reversal, not unlike Marx's prediction of the revolutionary turn that would be 'necessary' once everyone, save one or a few, were reduced to the condition of the proletariat. There seems to be no justification for the reversal of an 'extreme' condition into its opposite. Certainly, in Marx everything depends on the conditions of exploitation becoming intolerable and the fact that, ultimately, the proletariat has nothing to lose but its chains. However, it may be that the Marxian theory of the inevitability of revolution has been discredited because the reversal cannot be thought of in such mechanical terms (although it is clearly also linked to the fact that the universalization of the proletariat has not been linear and has itself followed the detours of symbolization). What one discovers in the disclosure of the violence of historical processes is the power of symbolization: not simply that everything is purely a play of forces, but that this play operates only if it is 'presented' in the form of a 'conflict of interpretations', that is, in the production of meaning. However, the production of meaning – and we are still with Nietzsche here – is only possible because man is an animal capable of 'taking sides against itself'.[8] The capacity to transcend the interests of survival that is characteristic of humanity and makes of it a cosmic event, 'pregnant with a future' (as Nietzsche writes on the same page of *The Genealogy of Morals*), is manifest not only in ascesis but above all in symbolic production in general (without which force won't 'work'). This nexus of disenchantment, the power of symbols and the capacity to transcend the impulse

Disenchantment and Dissolution

towards survival, is the meaning of the conclusion to another fine Nietzschean text that redescribes disenchantment and nihilism under the mantle of knowledge. In *The Twilight of the Idols*, Nietzsche shows 'how the "real world" at last became a fable', that is, how, from the world of Platonic ideas to the eternal life of Christianity to the Kantian a priori and Spencer's unknowable, the idea that beneath reality there may be a structure that is true, the source of certainty at the epistemological level and of norms at the moral level, withers to the point of dissolution. The 'real world' shows itself to be a fable. But, as this is the conclusion, 'with the real world we have also abolished the apparent world'. If there is no longer a true world to serve as a criterion, then even the apparent world will no longer be able to call itself by that name. Disenchantment, then, can be understood neither as the grasp of a true structure of reality, nor, and this is important, as a 'transposition' into a world of undisguised relations, that is, of pure relations of forces. Rather, Nietzsche thinks – even if the obscurity of this solution constitutes the true difficulty, perhaps irresolvable, of his late thought – in terms of a capacity for producing symbols that are not 'ideological', that is, not unwittingly functions of the establishment and maintenance of relations of domination. What is clear from his texts, however, is that the possibility of an activity that is symbolic of 'freedom' in this way is directly linked to the fact that humanity, withdrawn from the limits set by the struggle for existence and the blind will to live spoken of by Schopenhauer, can transcend the concern for survival.

It is not a matter here of being historically correct about what Nietzsche really had in mind, but rather of clarifying what he means for us, what he tells us about

Disenchantment and Dissolution

the problem of how to think disenchantment radically. Seen in this light, Nietzsche's thought suggests that disenchantment be understood as *something different from the discovery of equality, or communicative reciprocity, resulting from the exposure of metaphysics*. In itself, such an exposure could indeed lead to the discovery of equality. But one cannot rule out that, as Nietzsche himself concluded in many passages contrasting with the ideal of 'moderation' mentioned earlier, the consequence may be a pure and simple liberation of forces – and so of the will to violence and oppression.

If the exposure of ideology stops here, the problem of founding the right to propose new orders of meaning in something other than pure force remains unresolved. In Marx, for example, the right of the proletariat to guide history lies in the fact that it embodies the generic essence of man as well as representing the majority of humanity. In Marx, too, one can perhaps discover something analogous to the 'Schopenhauerism' discernible (amongst many contrasting signs) in the late Nietzsche, and which becomes explicit in thinkers like Horkheimer and Adorno. Indeed, it may be that in the final analysis the fact that the proletariat constitutes the vast majority of humanity is no guarantee that it is in the right (this would merely be another way of recognizing force). Nor is the fact that, as itself expropriated, it could embody the true essence of humanity, broken down (Rousseau) by social mechanisms, property and the false consciousness of ideology. Rather, let us say that there may be reason to suppose the proletariat is in the right on the basis of the fact that, as expropriated, it has been 'reduced' to the existential, to that 'presque rien' Adorno talks about in the final chapter of *Negative Dialectics* as the last possible name of metaphysical being[9] – essential, with an evanscent air of the 'quintessential', a kind of slightness.

Not to betray disenchantment also means to recognize that it cannot stop at having simply established communicative reciprocity and equality amongst individuals, that is, liberalism. With all due respect to 'liberal' values – whose only drawback, as Habermas ultimately believes, is that they cannot be realized within the structures of bourgeois liberal society – there are stumbling-blocks in proposing that the left simply re-endorse them, and these obscure any awareness that, with the rediscovery of 'equal rights' at the end of disenchantment, we do nothing but ratify the world as 'will to power'. The attention given by the left today to a thinker such as Levinas seems to provide ample testimony to this. Levinas does not talk about the 'Other' in terms of reciprocity and equality; he thinks the Other to be a trace of Infinity, commanding our respect solely by virtue of being able to appeal to an 'Other' that transcends us all.

The critique of ideology and the dissolution of metaphysics, according to the 'praxial' reading exemplified by Löwith's text with which we began, may not be sufficient for the 're-foundation' of the left. We have here a kind of theoretical parallel to what we have seen happen many times at the political level: the left believes it can 're-found' itself by inheriting liberal theories and programmes, perhaps with their feet back on the ground. I shall not discuss the legitimacy of this procedure 'in general' here, for it is certainly also true that the political thinking and praxis of the 'left' – whatever that may mean now – assume the form of a 'secularizing' revival of the legacy of bourgeois thought. Nevertheless it may be that closer attention to what such a process of secularization means would probably lead us to follow the 'Schopenhauerian' pointers in Nietzsche. Given the 'strange' popularity of a thinker like Levinas in left-wing culture, along with the undeniable difficulties in Foucault's thought (is the archaeology of knowledge simply the exposure of *epistemai* as effects of the play of forces – and nothing besides?), and phenomena such as the attention given, by the left again, to Carl Schmitt's decisionism (the reduction of politics to the 'elementary' friend/foe relation is assuredly a form of disenchantment – but is it enough?), it would appear that the left has need of an injection of nihilism, or ethics. Moreover, I do not believe these are traits that come from the outside, as though introduced by chance. One can recommend fidelity to them in the same way that one can recommend being faithful to the choices of modernity. Indeed, one can do so with even greater rational 'cogency', at least in the sense that if modernity has opted for the egalitarian reading, as Flores rightly maintains, this choice includes, implicitly but unequivocally, a rejection of violence and oppression. But such a rejection requires that equality, as the meaning of disenchantment, be accompanied by an explicit commitment to the 'weakening' of being, that is, for a thought that openly attempts to locate itself outside the logic of the struggle for survival, or the liberal vision of the affirmation of rights in competition with each other. It is hard to see what the implications may be. But it is fairly clear that in a disenchanted world – from which God has been exiled, at least in his capacity as guarantor of the given objective order – disenchantment either drives itself to the point where it 'ironizes' even 'over ourselves' (the expression is again Nietzsche's), and so distances itself even from the 'will to live', or it has no

Disenchantment and Dissolution

argument whatsoever to counterpose to the reduction of social life to the pure and simple struggle of all against all.

Needless to say, I hope, it is not a matter of preaching a nihilistic morality in the negative sense of the term, rejected by Nietzsche as passive or 'reactive' nihilism. Even Schopenhauer did not preach suicide, for example, but rather a compassion and solidarity towards living beings that cannot be founded on their 'rights' – which are always likened to the affirmation of a will to live that sooner or later reveals itself to be inevitably competitive – but only on a kind of vocation to the 'dissolution' that emerges as a feature of the very disenchantment from which modernity was born.

It may be that there are no immediate and relevant consequences for concrete political programmes, although one could say that it is no small matter to introduce the notion of 'compassion' to the culture of the left, and in general to replace the critique of ideology with an explicit commitment to ethics as the capacity to transcend the logic of the struggle for life. Modern disenchantment, moreover, seems necessarily to open itself to the 'weak' dimension of dissolution, precisely insofar as it shows itself to be increasingly less tenable as the sole horizon of a philosophy of history. If we are to be faithful to the modern legacy of disenchantment, we shall probably have to give more careful consideration to this dimension.

NOTES

1 P. Flores d'Arcais, 'Il disincanto tradito', *Micromega* (Rome), 1586, n. 2.
2 K. Löwith, 'Gott, Mensch und Welt in der Metaphysik

Disenchantment and Dissolution

von Descartes bis zu Nietzsche', in *Samtliche Schriften*, vol. 9): *Gott, Mensch und Welt in der Philosophie der Neuzeit – G. B. Vico – Paul Valéry* (J. B. Metzlersche Verlagsbuchhandlung, Stuttgart, 1986).

3   Ibid.

4   Flores d'Arcais, 'Il disincanto', p. 91.

5   It seems to me that this 'formalist' turn is taken by both K. O. Apel in *Transformation der Philosophie*, 2 vols. (Suhrkamp Verlag, Frankfurt a. M., 1973) and J. Habermas, most recently in *The Theory of Communicative Action*, tr. T. McCarthy (Beacon Press, Boston, 1985). I have discussed the positions of Apel and Habermas more fully in my *Al di là del soggetto* (Feltrinelli, Milan, 1981).

6   F. Nietzsche, *Nachgelassene Fragmente: Herbst 1885 bis 1887*, in Werke vol. 8, 1. (Walter de Gruyter, Berlin/New York, 1974), pp. 215–21.

7   On this point, cf. my *Introduzione a Nietzsche* (Laterza, Bari, 1986), pp. 94ff.

8   F. Nietzsche, *The Genealogy of Morals* (1887), tr. W. Kaufmann and R. J. Hollingdale (Random House, New York, 1967), p. 85.

9   T. W. Adorno, *Negative Dialectics*, tr. E. B. Ashton (Routledge & Kegan Paul, London, 1973), pp. 395.

8

Ethics of Communication or Ethics of Interpretation?

The reasons one might have for saying that hermeneutics is distinctly inclined towards ethics seem at the same time to stand in the way of such an inclination being fully expressed. For the most part, it is only after *Truth and Method* that Gadamer began to emphasize the significance of hermeneutics as practical philosophy. Yet it is fairly clear to anyone familiar with this work that ethics is already one of its essential themes. Indeed, it may be that the increasingly central position of hermeneutics in the present philosophical scene depends precisely on its orientation towards ethics and the way it affirms ethics as a positive element in the critique of traditional metaphysics and of the scientism that is its most recent configuration. The term 'ethics' is used here in the narrow sense, and so in distinction from morality. Indeed, the horizon within which *Truth and Method* proclaimed the significance of truth in those fields of experience which are irreducible to the positive sciences, and which even 'include' these very sciences as a moment or part of themselves, was precisely that of sociality thought as 'reason in act', as *logos*, given primarily in the natural language of a determinate

Ethics of Communication or Interpretation?

historical community. The horizon is that of ethics, *qua* ethos, custom, the shared culture of an epoch and a society, and that which ultimately 'belies' scientism and its purported reduction of truth to single statements experimentally confirmed via the methodology of mathematical and natural science. Many of the trends of current thought may be found in this line of critique, whose encapsulation by *Truth and Method* became emblematic for the whole of contemporary philosophy. These include not only the 'critical' positions which, taking up Hegel and Marx, situate the truth of science within an historico-dialectical horizon oriented towards an emancipatory *telos*, but also all the developments of the Wittgensteinian doctrine of language games as expressions of 'forms of life', the Foucauldian archaeology of knowledge, with its notion of *epistemai* as historical horizons determined not by theoretical reason but by the play of forces and disciplinary decisions, and finally the conception of science's progression within the framework of paradigms for the most part determined otherwise than 'theoretically', which is the kernel of Thomas Kuhn's theory.

As the philosophically richest and most consistent expression and interpretation of the anti-scientific fever, hermeneutics is constituted from the very beginning as a philosophy led by an inclination for ethics (in the sense mentioned above). It has therefore contributed greatly to what has been called the 'rehabilitation of practical philosophy'. Yet the substance of this rehabilitation does not seem to satisfy the more specifically moral demands implied by ethics, its need to do justice to the expectation of norms and imperatives. The ethics that hermeneutics makes possible seems to be primarily an ethics of goods, to use Schleiermacher's expression, more than an ethics of imperatives. Or better still, if

Ethics of Communication or Interpretation?

there is an ethics delineated in hermeneutics, it is one in which, taking interpretation as an act of translation (Habermas, too, has spoken of philosophy's function as *Dolmetscher*), the various *logoi* – discourses of specialized languages, but also spheres of interest, regions of 'autonomous' rationality – are to be referred back to the *logos*-common consciousness, to the cradling substratum of values shared by a living historical community and expressed in its language. (This, incidentally, is the sense, the only sense possible, that an author like Donald Davidson, of 'analytic' formation yet open to the reasoning of hermeneutics, believes one has still to grant metaphysics; that of bringing out, through analyses of the language that we speak, the structures which hold fast, and by which our experience of the world is articulated.)[1] To be sure, according to this view, ethics seems to be static (or simply reactionary, and at least traditionalist), and this impression is reinforced the more one forgets – as Gadamer does *not* – that the bounds of the *logos*, of the common language-consciousness within which we are thrown and to which we must appeal in 'rationalizing' our choices, cannot be rigidly defined. Indeed, and this is simply another aspect of hermeneutics as koine, it seems that reason can be recognized as the *logos*-common consciousness only today, when natural languages, and the historical communities that speak them and that are spoken by them, are beginning to lose all stable boundaries and fixed identities. Accordingly, we must recognize that if Gadamer (above all in the essays in *Reason in the Age of Science*) understands the Socratic 'leap into the *logoi*' as the transition to the *logos*-common consciousness from specialist languages and particular spheres of interest (which become ethically reprehensible when they prevail in isolation), he can do so only insofar as the horizon of reference, the *logos* understood as reason in act in language, increasingly becomes only a limited idea, the regulative ideal of a community that is always in the course of making itself and which can never be identified with a factual historical society, whose established values would have to be accepted as canonical.

The conservative and reactionary appearance of the ethics inspired by hermeneutics thereby reveals itself to be, in fact, merely an appearance. Yet, and for these very same reasons, the transition to the *logos*-common consciousness, as a normative moral ideal, seems to be reduced to too little. To the precise extent that it is not thought of as an inherited body of values defined once and for all, this *logos* is ultimately identified with the pure and simple demand for universalization that philosophy raises formally, but to whose contents, meanings and actual criteria for choice it seems unwilling to commit itself. On the face of it, this amounts to a recognition that the values on the basis of which a preference is sometimes declared in social dialogue for one choice over another are radically historical. This is clearly right. But in considering itself a kind of meta-theory or meta-ethics, this philosophy represents itself to itself as non-historical, illusorily placed in an external viewpoint (a 'view from nowhere', as the title of a recent work by Thomas Nagel has it). Such a viewpoint does not exist, at least not if the hypothesis of a radical historicality characterizing the *logos* and the values by which it is constituted holds true.

What I propose to call an ethics of communication, in contrast to an ethics of interpretation, falls entirely within such a perspective still dominated by a transcendental-metaphysical prejudice whose view of historicality is by no means radical enough, at least from the point of view of hermeneutics. In spite of the undeniable differences, brought out in discussions and polemics, separating hermeneutics in its canonical Gadamerian form from the ethics of communication of writers such as Apel and Habermas, these positions are not really so far apart. To be precise, Apel and Habermas make explicit a transcendental attitude that Gadamer rejects, but which nonetheless remains as an almost unavoidable risk for his philosophy, at least insofar as he seems to refuse a radical recognition of the historicality of hermeneutics itself. In other words, the ethics inspired by hermeneutics, at least in its Gadamerian formulation, is faced by only two paths. It either ossifies, and determines the physiognomy of the *logos* unambiguously as the ensemble of values shared by an actual historical community (articulating itself, perhaps, as 'semantic metaphysics' in the style of Davidson), in which case it inevitably becomes a conservative ethic, taking accepted values and the existing order as its criteria; or else, as tends to happen on the whole, it recognizes the *logos*-language in actual conditions as a limit-idea, and ultimately presents itself as a pure demand for universalization via communication, not unlike that which is heard, in the light of an explicit return to Kant, in Apel and Habermas.

As we have remarked, from the point of view of hermeneutics, these positions propose, at least implicitly, the restoration of metaphysics. This is not solely, or not so much, because the subject whose transparency is to be promoted (against the opacity of an existence conditioned by the division of labour, neuroses, various forms of institutional violence, etc.) is modelled on the subject of metaphysics and modern scientism, whose ultimate form is that of full self-consciousness. Above all, it is because the normative ideal of unrestricted communication displays its categorical character in its recognition of an essential structure, holding for every historical experience, but itself withdrawn from becoming. Despite not insignificant differences in their views, Apel and Habermas agree in recognizing that experience is made possible, in the final analysis, by the a priori of unrestricted communication or communicative action. As the condition for the possibility of experience, it is also, immediately and according to the classical overturning of being (permanent, structural) into value, the norm for action. In Habermas, this overturning is less evident than in Apel, since it occurs by way of a more explicit affirmation of the 'intersubjective' essence of the I. Moreover, it involves an articulation of forms of action into different levels, where the norm seems to be delineated as a respect for the rules proper to each level (these are ultimately the Crocian distinctions, and the games of Wittgenstein as well), in opposition to unwarranted attempts at 'colonization'. In reality, however, the overriding imperative is that of communicability. There is no illegitimate colonization of other levels by communicative action; only the opposite is conceivable. The 'intersubjective' essence of the I, then, does not bind the I to concrete historical conditions, but is affirmed only as a function of the specific normativity of the 'collective' as the site of communication-universalization. As Dieter Henrich has observed, this constitutive aspect of Habermas's theory reflects the typically modern persuasion 'that a human life reaches stillness and perfection only when in its praxis it finds the way towards that community of men which came before it'.[2] Whereas, for example, the young Hegel, and many more recent theorists, conceive this process of self-discovery in the community in more intimate terms, such as love, Habermas thinks of it in terms of political existence and rational discussion. But, going beyond Henrich's intentions, we could add that even this confirms, if there were any need (and Habermas certainly does not deny it), the profound link between the ethics of communication and modern metaphysics, oriented towards the full explication of the subject. This explication never ceases to be couched in Cartesian terms as self-transparency, even when associated with the idea of community. Indeed, the latter is (even as the myth of the organic community) the self-transparency of the subject translated onto the social plane.

Habermas believes that by affirming the intersubjective constitution of the I he is doing justice to the finitude of the subject and breaking with idealism, understood primarily as creeping solipsism (his objections to Adorno may be seen in *Theory of Communicative Action*). In reality, however, his principal concern is to reflect the finitude of the subject which results from its having become an object of positive knowledge. The finitude that Habermas guarantees the subject is therefore only that which belongs to objects of science,[3] and not that of historical existence. The decisive weight that Habermas assigns to positive research in linguistics, psychology and sociology (Mead, Piaget) when constructing the theory of communicative action has its roots here. From the point of view of critical theory, too, one would have to question the extent to which Habermas remains faithful to his own presuppositions, given that he appeals to the results of these human sciences without giving a thought to their historicality – such as their belonging to a certain *episteme* (in Foucault's sense) or to a configuration of social relations of domination (in the classical Marxist sense). In any case, such a 'scientistic' expression of finitude in the face of idealist metaphysics cannot correspond to

Ethics of Communication or Interpretation?

the genuine intentions of hermeneutics, which must recognize its own distance from the ethics of communication. By contrast, hermeneutics 'deposes' the idealist subject, but not in order to lay it open to investigation by the positive sciences. For Habermas, the fact that the I is 'ascribed' to its relations with others means that it is finite insofar as it can thereby become the object of the human sciences. For hermeneutics, that the I is ascribed to intersubjective constitution (or, with Heidegger, 'thrown' into a world) means that nothing that concerns it can be the object of structural description, but may be given only as destiny. To be sure, the human sciences may form a part of this destiny as well, but in this case they are presented in a very different light. There may be no objection to Habermas's presupposition, more or less implicit, that it is the extension of the sciences to knowledge of humanity that characterizes modernity and obliges philosophy to change direction. However, this cannot be taken as the ultimate manifestation, via scientific method, of the true constitution of human existence (whereby, for Habermas, the human sciences in some way 'prove' the intersubjective essence of the I). If one wishes to execute the turn modernity demands of thought, one must renounce the metaphysical ideal of knowledge as the description of objectively given structures. Habermas's intersubjective I is wholly the I of modern metaphysics-science. It is the object of the human sciences and the equally ahistorical subject of the laboratory.

These ahistorical traits are such that the ethics of communication cannot be considered a fitting outcome for the moral inclination of hermeneutics. In fact, the latter has sought, for ethical reasons, to affirm historicality as *belonging*: the experience of truth does not occur in the reflection of an object by a subject committed to self-transparency, but rather as the articulation – or interpretation – of a tradition (a language, a culture), to which existence belongs, and which it reformulates in new messages sent to other interlocutors. Ethical life and historicality coincide here. Hermeneutics can live up to its ethical inclination in an appropriate fashion only by remaining faithful to the instance of historicality. But how? Principally, by thinking of itself not as an ultimately metaphysical descriptive theory of the hermeneutic constitution of existence, but rather as an event of destiny. Hermeneutics must recognize itself as the thought belonging to the epoch of the end of metaphysics, and nothing more. Hermeneutics is not the adequate description of the human condition, which is finally making headway only at a certain point in history, thanks to a particular thinker or a series of fortuitous circumstances. It is the philosophical thought of secularized Europe. The fact that its source lies in the world of the Protestant Reformation, the religious wars, the classicist dream of a recovery of the tradition of literature and art of antiquity, is far more important for hermeneutics than is generally recognized. In 'Habermasian' terms, we could translate: hermeneutics is the philosophy of the society of public opinion, of mass media. In Heideggerian vernacular: it is the philosophy of the epoch of world views and their inevitable conflict. These various characterizations – which could easily be multiplied, indeed which *must* be multiplied – respond to a question that arises directly from the originary core of hermeneutics. If it theorizes that the experience of truth is belonging and not reflection, it must also say to which epoch, world or provenance it itself as theory belongs. It cannot lie back, believing itself to have finally presented an adequate description of existence, of its interpretative constitution. Within these bounds, hermeneutics would appear as a hopelessly banal metaphysical theory, even as the most banal and futile. In fact, it says that there is no such thing as truth as a stable structure of being reflected in propositions, but only many horizons and the many different cultural horizons within which experiences of truth occur, as internal articulations or interpretations. Even if we go further still, singling out the regulative ideal of promoting dialogue between different horizons and cultural universes, we do not get far; *what* will hermeneutics have to say once dialogue has been established?

If, however, the 'trivial' and weak hermeneutic thesis recognizes itself as *belonging*, instead of disguising itself as a metaphysical description, then it will see itself as a destiny (a provenance) and will become capable of choice, that is, of morality. Hermeneutics will recognize its destiny, if it understands the *nihilistic* character of its constitution. Even for hermeneutics itself as theory, truth does not consist in reflecting a given fact, but in responding to a destiny. This destiny is that of the epoch of the end of metaphysics, in which, as Heidegger says, the first lightning flash of the event of being lights up inasmuch as in this moment man and being lose the characteristics ascribed to them by metaphysics (which is the thought of presence, of objectivity, of the will to power). Hermeneutics – and this would have to be discussed examining the mode of argument, rich and dense, but also very *rusé* and elusive, that Gadamer employs in *Truth and Method* – cannot but legitimate itself as corresponding to a destiny that we call modernity; it certainly cannot see itself as an adequate description of some kind of structure of existence. In simple terms, one can say that if there is any reason for listening to the discourse of hermeneutics, it can only lie

Ethics of Communication or Interpretation?

in the fact that hermeneutics is presented as belonging to the age in which we live, as its theory, and so only in a certain sense 'adequate'.[4] It is in the world of public opinion, of the mass media, of Weberian 'polytheism', of the technical and potentially total organization of existence, that a theory of truth not as correspondence but as interpretation may be found. A more explicit articulation of this destiny, of the fact that it itself belongs to modernity (even defined in terms of nihilism and the oblivion of being) is a task that hermeneutics has yet to complete. Gadamer chose not to give this sense to his discourse, and in the final analysis this precludes him from taking hermeneutics as destiny, with the ethical consequences that we have noted above. He seems to have thought rather that it was a matter of proclaiming the possibility of extra-methodic experiences of truth, in opposition to the claims of modern scientism, which became exclusive only after Kant, and of putting forward an idea of truth as belonging that was already known to the Greeks and which can still be traced as a minor theme in modernity. Here, too, is the source of the greater friendliness shown by Gadamer than by Heidegger towards metaphysics, which does not seem to him at all marked by an irremediable and nihilistic forgetfulness of being. From a rigorously Heideggerian standpoint, hence one that is radically faithful to the historicality at the origin of hermeneutics, the latter cannot seriously take itself to be an alternative to modernity, since this would require that it legitimate itself as founded on some *evidence* that modernity had neglected or forgotten. Instead, it must present itself as the thought of the epoch of the end of metaphysics, that is, as the thought of modernity and its consummation, and nothing more. Now Heidegger teaches us that modernity is accomplished as nihilism, *Ge-stell*, the world of

Ethics of Communication or Interpretation?

technological and scientific rationalization, the world of the conflict between the *Weltbilder*. This is the world in which *Ereignis* 'flashes', in which there is a chance to overcome metaphysics and its objectifying mentality,[5] precisely because humanity and being lose their metaphysical qualities, above all those of subject and object. In what sense, though, can it be said more specifically that hermeneutics, as that thought which places itself outside metaphysics, is made possible by modernity itself as universal technological domination and the accomplishment of nihilism? In the first place, such a thesis seems to conflict with explicit remarks made by Heidegger, who only rarely (such as in the text on the flash of *Ereignis* which appears in *Identity and Difference*), allows a glimpse of the possibility that the nihilistic traits of modernity itself may herald a new thought that is no longer metaphysical. This possibility, only glimpsed by Heidegger, might become explicit and recognizable only with the profound modification undergone by *Gestell*, the world of the technical, with the transition from mechanical technology to information technology. It is well known that today the distinction between developed and underdeveloped countries is no longer made in terms of the possession of mechanical technology capable of bending, concentrating and overcoming the forces of nature, of shifting, dismantling and rebuilding. It is no longer a question of engines, but of computers and the networks connecting them which make it possible to control the more 'primitive' machines, that is, the mechanical ones. It is not in the world of machines and engines that humanity and being can shed the mantles of subject and object, but in the world of generalized communication. Here the entity dissolves in the images distributed by the information media, in the abstraction of scientific objects (whose correspondence

Ethics of Communication or Interpretation?

with real 'things' open to experience can no longer be seen) or technical products (that do not even make contact with the real world via their use value, since the demands they satisfy are increasingly artificial). Whereas the subject, on its part, is less and less a centre of self-consciousness and decision-making, reduced as it is to being the author of statistically predicted choices, playing a multiplicity of social roles that are irreducible to a unity. In the *Ge-stell* of information, the world of images of the world, the true world, as Nietzsche said, becomes a fable; or, to use the Heideggerian term, *Sage*. Hermeneutics is the philosophy of this world in which being is given in the form of weakening or dissolution. The thesis 'there are no facts, only interpretations' has a reductive sense, of the loss of reality, which is essential to hermeneutics.

On the ethical plane, the effect of all this is to replace an ethics of communication with an ethics of interpretation. The former, as we have seen, singled out the norm of unrestricted communication, or communicative action, only at the price of placing itself in a substantially ahistorical position. Moreover, it pays for this choice by leading, on the one hand, to an oscillation between formalism and cultural relativism, and, on the other, to a dependency on the modern ideal of the subject, the subject of science (in both senses of the genitive). By contrast, in the classical Heideggerian definition interpretation means the 'articulation of what is understood', the unfolding of a knowledge in which existence is always already thrown, according to its destining: primarily, then, to look for the guiding criteria of choice in the provenance and not in a structure of existence, not even the hermeneutic structure. Hermeneutics, as an awareness that truth is not reflection but belonging, is not born out of the correction of an error, or the rectification of a perspective. It arises from modernity as the epoch of metaphysics and of its accomplishment in the nihilism of the *Ge-stell*. Recognizing its own nihilistic destiny, hermeneutics paves the way for an ethics founded on an ontology of reduction and dilution – or, if one prefers, of dissolution. In this ethics is a convergence of several Schopenhauerian elements to be found in the most familiar moral precepts of our century: the experimentalism of the later Nietzsche, for whom the overman was at bottom the 'more moderate' man, the artist even, who loves experimentation even beyond the interests of his own self-preservation; the outcome of Adorno's negative dialectic (the *presque rien*, the culmination of the metaphysical *promesse de bonheur* in aesthetic appearance, conceived in terms of unreality and Kantian disinterest). But here, too, is an echo of the old Socratic teaching, of the daimon who speaks only to restrain and to say no.

Accepting its own nihilistic destiny, and inspired by an ontology of reduction – which carries to its natural conclusion the Heideggerian idea of being that can never be given as full presence, but only as trace and memory (and which thus cannot provide a foundation, authority, sovereignty) – hermeneutics eludes a further risk that does not seem entirely ruled out by the ethics of communication. The latter can in fact try to avoid the accusation of still being a transcendental metaphysics (which posits as a normative foundation of morality the *fact* that experience is made possible by the a priori of unlimited communication) by stressing the pure formality of its conception; it excludes all metaphysical rigidity to the extent that it conceives morality to be negotiation, persuasion by way of rational argumentation, not limited by any necessary metaphysical structure. In this respect, the ethics of communication

Ethics of Communication or Interpretation?

presents itself as a rigorously egalitarian ethics. But at the same time, it shows itself unable to exclude the possibility that the egalitarianism and the negotiation come to be understood in the sense of a pure escalation of social conflict. Why, in the end, if there are no metaphysical principles, should we prefer rational argumentation to physical confrontation? (The hypothesis put forward here is not so preposterous; at times Foucault thinks of truth as the disciplinary event, the effect of a play of forces.) Habermas would respond that the method of rational argument is the most favourable to life and its development (nonetheless it is always a hypothetical imperative: if we want to live . . .). Alternatively, he would reply, shifting ground slightly, by theorizing that man is 'by nature' an intersubjective and communicative I (yet the only proof he offers for this thesis rests on the human sciences, which, as sciences, belong within a historical horizon that would be open to the most explicit thematic criticism, such as that offered by the original critical theory). However paradoxical it may seem, there is in the ethics of communication no sufficient 'foundation' for morality. Again paradoxically, it is the ethics of interpretation that furnishes morality with the more substantial rationale – though not, to be sure, with a foundation. To the extent that hermeneutics recognizes itself as provenance and destiny, as the thought of the final epoch of metaphysics and thus of nihilism, it can find in 'negativity', in dissolution as the 'destiny of Being', given not as presence of the *arche* but only as provenance, the orienting principle that enables it to realize its own original inclination for ethics whilst neither restoring metaphysics nor surrendering to the futility of a relativistic philosophy of culture.

NOTES

1. Cf. D. Davidson, *Inquiries into Truth and Interpretation*, (Clarendon Press, Oxford, 1984), pp. 199–200.
2. D. Henrich, 'Was ist Metaphysik – Was ist Moderne?' *Merkur* (1986), pp. 495–508, esp. pp. 503–4.
3. On this cf. also Habermas's essay 'Rückkehr zur Metaphysik. Eine Tendenz der deutschen Philosophie?', *Merkur* (1985), pp. 898–905.
4. On these issues, see the essays collected in G. Vattimo (ed.), *Filosofia 86*, (Laterza, Bari, 1987).
5. May I refer the reader to my essay on 'Metafisica, violenza, secolarizzazione', in *Filosofia 86*.

Index

Absolute Spirit, 6, 7, 18, 21
Adorno, Theodor, 5, 6, 23, 46–8, 58, 63, 64, 74, 78, 80–2, 86–7, 96, 100, 104, 111, 118
advertising, 22
aesthetics, 9, 10, 45–60, 62–5, 66–73, 85, 118
alienation, 37, 54, 56, 58–9
Allen, Woody, 84
ambiguity (in aesthetics) 59–60
analysis, of language, 107
  scientific, 17
anthropology, 10, 13, 14, 28, 31–3, 38, 67
anticapitalism, 33
anxiety, 50, 54, 58
Apel, K. O., 18–21, 24, 27, 104, 109, 110
archaism, 31–5, 37, 39
arche, 119
argumentation, rational, 118–19

Aristotle, 13, 46, 52, 53, 79
art, 2, 3, 10, 29, 31, 45–60, 62–4, 66, 68, 70, 71, 76, 113, 118
  and see aesthetics
artificiality, 117
Aufklärung, 23
Auf-stellung, 52–3
  and see foundation, founding
aura (in art), 46, 89
Auschwitz, 81
authoritarianism, 94–5
avant-garde, 31, 63–4

Bacon, Francis, 79
banality, 10, 54, 57
Barilli, R., 74
Barthes, Roland, 28
Bauhaus school, 64
beauty, the beautiful, 52, 53, 62, 66–72
Beckett, Samuel, 63
Beethoven, Ludwig van, 69

Index

Being, 10–11, 45, 50, 52, 55, 56, 61
belonging, 10, 112–14, 117
Bengodi (imaginary country), 79
Benjamin, Walter, 2, 45–9, 51–6, 58, 60, 63, 73, 81, 89
Bible, the, 42, 51, 80
'Big Brother', 5, 6, 10
Blade Runner (film), 83
Bloch, Ernst, 47, 63, 64, 74, 80, 81, 89
bourgeoisie
 culture, 31
 values, 101

Campanella, T., 79
capitalism, 5, 6, 31–4, 41, 82, 88, 93
Cassirer, E., 24, 27, 29, 30, 43
catastrophes, effect of, 83–5
catharsis, 47, 52, 53
causality, principle of, 79
centralization, 2–5, 9
Christ, Jesus, 2, 3, 41, 42
Christianity, 41, 87–8, 99
cinema, 36, 47, 48, 49, 51, 76–7
cinematography, 83
civilization, 2–3, 41–2, 46
classes, social, 3
classicism, 42, 73, 113
cogito, Cartesian, 43
collectionism, 70
collective, the, 12–13, 41, 110

colonialism, 4, 5, 32, 38
colonization, political, 4, 110
communication, 1, 4, 5–6, 9, 10, 12, 13–16, 48, 58, 60, 65, 105–19
 and see media
communism, 77
community, 18, 19, 20, 41, 67–70, 106–7, 110–11
computers, 116
Comte, Auguste, 6, 18, 41
conflict, social, 20, 119
conformity, 26
confrontation, physical, 119
consumer arts, 36
consumer objects, 48
conservatism, 109
contemporaneity, 16, 17
counter-finality (of reason), 78, 81–2, 87, 88
counter-utopia, 76–88
court, influence of, 3, 41
creativity, 2, 55, 57, 58, 60
Croce, Benedetto, 110
culture(s), 9, 10, 14, 17, 21, 28, 31, 32, 33, 37, 38, 58, 106

Dada (art movement), 49
daimon, Socratic, 118
Dante Alighieri, 51
Dasein, 50
Davidson, Donald, 107, 109, 120
death, 49–50
 and see mortality
decisionism, decision-

Index

making, 102, 117
dehumanization, 59
democracy, 92
demonic, the, 5
demystification (of religion), 40, 42
demythologization, 29, 39, 40, 42, 49, 70
desacralization, 41
Descartes, René, terminology of, 111
  and see cogito
design, ideology of, 62, 64
destiny, 112–15, 119
determination, materialist, 19
Dewey, John, 11, 62, 74
dialect(s), 8, 9, 10
dialectic, 19, 21, 86, 96, 106, 118
dialogue, 11, 26, 38
dictatorships, 5
Dilthey, W., 10, 23, 71, 75
disenchantment, 29, 90–103
disorientation, 8, 9, 10, 51–60
dissolution, 5, 103, 117–19
distortion, 41, 42, 87–8
dogmatism, 19, 26
Dolmetscher, philosophy as, 107
domination
  of nature, 15, 24
  political, 3, 22–3, 111
dreaming, 9, 40

egalitarianism, 94–5, 102
egocracy, 94–5

Elias, Norbert, 41, 44
emancipation, 2, 3, 4, 5, 7–10, 17, 18, 21, 23, 24, 26, 39–40, 42, 63, 65, 68, 78, 82, 106
engines, mechanical, 116
Enlightenment, the, 2, 3, 17, 66, 96
Entmythologisierung, 34
  and see demythologization
episteme, epistemai, 106, 111
epistemology, 17, 34
equality, 96, 101–2
  and see egalitarianism
Ereignis, 55, 56, 116
ethics, 9, 34, 88, 93, 95, 102–3, 105–19
ethnology, 10
evacuation, 41–2
evolution, 30
experimentalism, 118
explanation, causal, 23
expressionism, 31, 77, 81
expressivity, 65, 69

fable(s), 7, 99, 117
fabling, 24–6, 28
faith, fidelity, 93–5, 102
fascism, 33, 77, 97
film, 49, 51, 54, 58, 85
  and see cinema
finitude, 9, 111–12
Flores d'Arcais, P., 90–1, 93, 95, 96, 102, 103–4
flower children, 84
Foucault, M., 102, 106, 111, 119

Index

foundation, founding, 8, 52, 53, 58
France
  aesthetics in, 47
  'new right' in, 33
Frankfurt school, 32, 62
freedom, 6, 7, 10, 11
  in art, 60
  and see emancipation, liberation

Gadamer, H. G., 60, 66, 75, 105–6, 107, 109, 114, 115
games
  in art, 57
  language, 18, 19, 106, 110
Gay Science, The, (work by Nietzsche), 9, 40
Geborgenheit, 52–4
Gehlen, Arnold, 14, 89
Geisteswissenschaft, 38
Ge-stell, 55–6, 115–18
Girard, R., 41–2, 44
God, gods, 93, 95, 96–7, 102
grammar, 9
Greeks, ancient, 32, 51, 115
Gulliver's Travels, 76
Gutenberg Galaxy, the, 15

Habermas, Jürgen, 13, 18, 21, 24, 27, 65, 66, 68, 74, 101, 104, 107, 109, 110–12, 119, 120
'happening' (in art), 45
harmony (in art), 46–7, 53, 54, 57, 63

Hegel, G. W. F., 3, 6, 7, 13, 21, 41, 46, 52, 62, 80, 86, 106,
  and see Absolute Spirit
Hegelianism, 23, 80
Heidegger, Martin, 7, 8, 10, 11, 15, 16, 23, 27, 33–4, 41, 44–6, 49–56, 58–61, 71, 73–5, 78–9, 81, 86–7, 89, 93, 112–18
Heinrich, Dieter, 110–11, 120
hermeneutics, 18, 24, 26–7, 34, 38, 48, 60, 66, 87, 105–9, 112–19
Her-stellung, 52–3
heterotopia, 69–74
Hillman, J., 36, 43
historicality, 108, 112–13, 115
historicism, 4, 33, 41
historicity, 9
historiography, 22, 25, 36, 38, 71
history, 2–6, 9, 17, 21–4, 30–2, 36–9, 41, 42, 43, 67–8
  and see unilinearity
Hölderlin, J. C. F., 52
Holy Roman Empire, 4
Horkheimer, Max, 5, 78, 82, 96, 100
humanism, 59, 93
Huxley, Aldous, 77

ideal(s), 3, 4, 17, 19–25, 39, 47, 108

124

Index

ideas, Platonic, 99
image(s), 7, 8, 15, 16, 21, 36, 49, 51, 76, 79, 80, 116, 117
imperative(s), 18, 19, 106
imperialism, 4, 5, 6, 31, 32
information, 12–16, 22, 57
  and see media, news
interiorization, 41
interpretation(s), 7, 11, 25, 41, 48, 50, 105–19
intersubjective, the, 84–5, 87
irrationalism, tempered, 31, 35–6, 43
Italy
  cultural circles in, 47
  'new right' in, 33

Jung, Karl Gustav, 36

Kant, Emmanuel, 14, 18, 46, 52, 65–70, 109, 115, 118
Kitsch, 72
knowledge, 6, 7, 10, 17–18, 19, 25–6, 30, 32, 33, 35, 38
Kuhn, Thomas, 34, 43, 106

labour, division of, 63, 109
Lang, Fritz, 76
language, 9, 18–19, 106–8
  and see linguistics
Lefebvre, Henri, 63, 74
left (political), the, 32, 90, 92, 101–3
Lessing, G. E., 2, 6
Levinas, E., 101–2

Lévi-Strauss, C., 28–30, 32, 43
liberalism, 31, 33, 101, 102
liberation, 8, 9, 39, 54
limit-idea, 109
linguistics, 18, 19, 111
  and see hermeneutics, language
literature, 3, 29–30, 36, 76–7, 113
'logical socialism', 19
logic, hermeneutic, 26
logos, logoi, 30, 105, 107–9
love, 110
Löwith, Karl, 41, 92–3, 97, 101, 103
Lubbe, H., 89
Lukács, G., 32, 62–4
Lyotard, J.-F., 5

machinery, machines, 15, 116
McLuhan, Marshall, 14, 15
magic, 29
manipulation, 6, 16, 55–6, 59, 82
Marcuse, Herbert, 46, 62–4, 66, 74
market, effect of, 48, 70
  on art, 45
  on information, 6
Marquard, O., 34–5, 43
Marx, Karl, 3, 6, 7, 41, 98, 100, 106
Marxism, 4, 18, 62–4, 111
materialism, 19
mathematics, 106
Mead, Margaret, 111

125

Index

mechanics, mechanisms, 16, 23, 45
  and see machines
media, mass, 1, 4–7, 10, 14–15, 21, 26, 28, 36, 43, 46, 48, 56–7, 113, 116
metaphysics, 7–9, 21, 23, 30–1, 33, 37–9, 41–2, 53–4, 56, 59, 61, 79–81, 86–7, 95–7, 100–1, 109, 111, 113–16, 118
  and see philosophy
meta-rule, 18
meta-theory, 108
Miller, D. L., 43
models, 2, 23–5, 36, 40, 68–70
moderation, ideal of, 100
modernization, 14, 41–3
monopolies, 5
monotheism, 88
moral(s), 17, 18, 19, 93, 96–7, 108, 112, 118
morality, 18, 105
More, Thomas, 79
mortality, 56, 58
  and see death
music, 29–30, 48
myth(s), 8, 25, 26, 28–43, 68, 111
mythology, 28, 43

Nagel, Thomas, 108
narration, narrative, 25–6, 35–6, 38
Nature, 15–16, 24, 26, 31–2, 56, 97

Naturwissenschaft, 38
Nazism, 33, 69, 97
negativity, 77–8, 87, 119
necessity, 56
neo-Kantianism, 18
neuroses, 8, 109
news, 5, 12, 14, 17
  and see information, media
Nietzsche, F., 3, 7–11, 25–6, 33, 40, 42, 58, 64, 70, 75, 78, 81, 96–100, 102–4, 117–18
nihilism, 11, 48, 87, 96, 99, 102–3, 114–16, 118–19
non-violence, 95
nostalgia, 8, 11, 42, 57, 73, 84–6
novelties (in art), 57

objectification, scientific, 32, 38–9
objectivity, 7, 8, 19, 24, 25, 96–7, 112, 114, 116
oblivion (of being), 56
obstacles (to communication), 19, 20
Old Testament, *see* Bible
ontology, 15, 73
opacity, 19, 20, 109
orientation, 52
originality (in art), 2, 57
origins, 37, 39
ornament, 71–3
Orwell, George, 5, 76–7
  and see 'Big Brother'
oscillation, 7, 10, 11, 52–60

Index

paradigms, 34, 106
Peirce, C. S., 18, 19, 20, 24
philologists, 32
philosophy, 2–4, 8, 11, 14, 18–19, 26, 28, 31, 37–8, 43, 62, 71–2, 81
  and see metaphysics
phronesis, 53
Piaget, Jean, 111
Planet of the Apes, the (film), 83
Plato, 36, 43, 78, 99
  and see daimon, transcendence
plurality (of cultures etc.), 6, 9, 10, 26, 36, 38–9, 67, 69–70
poetry, 52, 60
politics, 9, 13, 28, 30, 59, 90, 92–3, 95, 102
polytheism, 36, 115
Popper, K. R., 24, 27
positivism, 3–4, 14, 18, 35, 39
post-apocalypse, 83–6, 88
postmodernity, 1–11, 42–3, 66
pragmatists, 11
praxis, 90–2, 101, 110
prejudice, 18, 19
presque rien, 118
progress, 2–3, 4, 28, 32, 37, 41–2, 81, 84–6
proletariat, 98, 100
proliferation (of views, information, images), 5, 6, 8

promesse de bonheur, 118
propaganda, 5, 23
Protestantism, 9, 88
  and see Reformation
Proust, Marcel, 43
psychoanalysis, 18, 20, 36, 43
psychology, 13, 14, 15, 17, 111

radicality (in art), 57
radio, 5, 7
rationalism, 34, 43, 78–80
rationality, 3, 7, 8, 9, 30, 34–6, 38–9, 118–19
rationalization, 43, 81–3, 85–7, 92–3, 96, 107
reality, 6, 7, 8, 10, 12, 17, 25, 29, 31, 59, 63, 94, 99
reason, 18, 21, 34, 37, 39, 40, 52, 65, 82, 87, 96
  and see counter-finality
reciprocity, communicative, 96, 100–1
recording (of music), 48
Reformation, Protestant, 113
relativism
  cultural, 31, 34–5, 38–9
  philosophy, 25, 119
religion, 9, 29, 40–2, 113
reorientation, 52, 60
reproduction, 46–8, 51, 54, 57, 79
researchers, community of, 24
responsibility, individual, 93

Index

revolution, revolutionary movements, 21, 36–7, 63–4, 66, 77
Ricoeur, Paul, 71
rights, affirmation of, 102, 103
right-wing (politics), 33, 37
ritual, 29
'rockers' (hooligans), 69
romanticism, 42, 52
Rousseau, J.-J., 100

sacred, the, 41–2, 87
Sage, 117
Sartre, J.-P., 21, 27, 32
scepticism, 25
Schleiermacher, F., 106
Schmitt, Carl, 102
Schoenberg, Arnold, 63
Schopenhauer, Arthur, 85, 97, 99–103, 118
science, 15, 16, 23–4, 29–30, 32, 38–9, 82, 84, 111
   and see technology
sciences, 69
   human, 12–27, 56, 111–12
   natural, 16, 18, 23–4, 39, 106
   nomothetic, 23
   positive, 56, 105, 112
   social, 16, 20–1, 28
   and see sociology
scientism, 18, 105, 106, 109, 111, 115
scientists, community of, 24
Scott, Ridley, 83
secularization, 40–1, 87–8, 101–2, 113
security, 41–2, 52, 54
self-awareness, self-consciousness, 6, 7, 17, 19, 109–10, 117
self-transparency, 17, 18, 21–4, 26, 111–12
sex, sexuality, 3, 9
sfondamento, 61
Shakespeare, W., 51
shock, *see Stoss*
Simmel, Georg, 55, 61
situationism, 59, 63–4
socialism, logical, 19, 20, 24
society, 1, 6, 12–27, 57, 108
sociology, 13, 23, 25, 36, 45–6, 58–9, 111
Socrates, 107 *and see* daimon
solipsism, 111
Sorel, G.-E., 28, 36
sovereign, the, 3, 41
Spencer, Herbert, 99
Spinoza, B. de, 7, 9
Stalinism, 77, 92
State, the, 13, 41
Stellen, 55
   and see Ge-stell
stories, 36, 43
Stoss (shock), 47–51, 53, 57–8
structuralism, 31–2, 72–3, 107, 112, 114, 118
superficiality (in art), 57, 59
subsystems, 67–9
superstition, 18, 54
surrealism, 31, 63
survival, impulse towards, 98–9

Index

'suspicion', school of, 26
symbol(s), 25–6, 36, 48, 57
symbolization, 98–9
syntax, 9

technology, 12, 13, 15, 16, 22–4, 32, 46, 48, 54–6, 77–9, 81–2, 92–3, 115–17
techno-science, 8, 31, 33
telematics, 5
teleology, 67
television, 5, 7, 12, 17, 36
 and see media
telos, 39, 80, 82, 106
theology, Hebraic-Christian, 41
theatre, 45
theory (v. praxis), 90–2
third world, 6, 31
Tönnies, F. J., 41
totalitarianism, 5, 6, 59, 77
tradition, 1, 31, 37, 40–1, 52
tragedy, Greek, 51
Tranfalgia, Nicola, 22, 27
transcendence, 14, 108, 118
 Platonic, 21
Traviata, La (opera), 69
truth, 19–20, 26, 34, 40, 42, 47, 51, 55, 112, 114, 115, 119

Urmensch, 10, 26
unfounding, 52–3, 57–8, 73
 and see *sfondamento*
Un-heimlichkeit, 50
unilinearity (of history), 2–6, 39, 67, 81, 87
United States, the, 5, 46
universality, 67–70
universalization, 108–9
Un-zu-Haus-sein, 50
utopia(s), 17, 33, 46, 62–74, 76–88

Valéry, Paul, 48
value, 15, 48–9
Vattimo, G., 27, 44, 60–1, 89, 120
Verra, V., 89
Verwindung, 41, 44, 75, 89
violence, 8, 41, 42, 98, 100, 102, 109

Wagner, Richard, 69
Weber, Max, 24, 30, 41, 82, 88, 89, 115
Wesen, 58
 and see Being
Windelband, W., 23
Wittgenstein, Ludwig, 11, 18, 106
Wölfflin, Heinrich, 24

zero-model, 24

ZP.P5